-7 FEB 2011
2 8 APR 2011
2 8 MAY 2011
2 2 MAR 2012

KT-430-970

C014693841

COUNTY COUNCIL

A Quick Start Guide to
ONLINE SELLING

NEW TOOLS
FOR
BUSINESS

A Quick Start Guide to
ONLINE SELLING

**Sell your product on eBay,
Amazon and other
online marketplaces**

Cresta Norris

KoganPage

LONDON PHILADELPHIA NEW DELHI

Publisher's note

Every possible effort has been made to ensure that the information contained in this book is accurate at the time of going to press, and the publishers and author cannot accept responsibility for any errors or omissions, however caused. No responsibility for loss or damage occasioned to any person acting, or refraining from action, as a result of the material in this publication can be accepted by the editor, the publisher or the author.

First published in Great Britain and the United States in 2010 by Kogan Page Limited

Apart from any fair dealing for the purposes of research or private study, or criticism or review, as permitted under the Copyright, Designs and Patents Act 1988, this publication may only be reproduced, stored or transmitted, in any form or by any means, with the prior permission in writing of the publishers, or in the case of reprographic reproduction in accordance with the terms and licences issued by the CLA. Enquiries concerning reproduction outside these terms should be sent to the publishers at the undermentioned addresses:

120 Pentonville Road	525 South 4th Street, #241	4737/23 Ansari Road
London N1 9JN	Philadelphia PA 19147	Daryaganj
United Kingdom	USA	New Delhi 110002
www.koganpage.com		India

© Cresta Norris, 2010

The right of Cresta Norris to be identified as the author of this work has been asserted by her in accordance with the Copyright, Designs and Patents Act 1988.

ISBN   978 0 7494 6159 1
E-ISBN   978 0 7494 6160 7

British Library Cataloguing-in-Publication Data

A CIP record for this book is available from the British Library.

Library of Congress Cataloging-in-Publication Data

Norris, Cresta.
   A quick start guide to online selling : sell your product on eBay, Amazon and other online marketplaces / Cresta Norris.
      p. cm.
   ISBN 978-0-7494-6159-1 – ISBN 978-0-7494-6160-7   1. Electronic commerce.
2. Selling.   3. Internet marketing.   4. Retail trade.   I. Title.
   HF5548.32.N65 2010
   658.8′72--dc22

                                                                              2010034266

Typeset by Graphicraft Limited, Hong Kong
Production managed by Jellyfish
Printed in the UK by CPI Antony Rowe

Hampshire County Library

C014693841	
Askews	Sep-2010
658.872	£9.99
	9780749461591

PART II Selling things large and small 51

PART III Selling intangibles: ideas and creativity 81

INTRODUCTION

Broke? Not paid enough in your present job? Your small business in the doldrums? Longing to buy a new car or revamp the living room?

Making money is easier than you think! You can do it in your pyjamas without leaving home. You don't need an office or a warehouse; a kitchen table serves to rest the laptop on, and a garage or an attic or the cupboard under the stairs might come in handy for storing products, but even those aren't essential. The only thing you need is an internet connection. Unlike 'bricks and mortar' business, the online world has low entry costs and requires no qualifications.

There are as many ways to make money online as there are creative people coming up with new ideas. It's not just about selling things; you can just as easily make money online by selling ideas. In this book you'll hear about some of the ingenious ways other people have used the internet to make money by selling products, services or the fruits of their imagination.

Oh, I don't know, you're saying nervously. I haven't any creative talent. I haven't any business experience. What if I get ripped off? I don't know what to sell. It looks so complicated, all those payment systems and seller's feedback ratings and...

Stop being negative and listen. It's really not difficult. There are grandmothers out there selling stuff on eBay. There are teenagers making money out of the music they recorded in their bedroom. You can make it as simple or as complicated as you want.

You could start with the contents of your attic – all those unwanted presents that are gathering dust.

You could turn a hobby into cash.

Or you could decide to set up an ambitious online retail operation to build on the success of an existing business.

Once you begin thinking like an online entrepreneur, the sky's the limit!

Making money is about an attitude of mind. You need to be hungry to see the opportunities. This book aims to waft a set of tempting aromas under your nostrils, to stimulate your appetite for online commerce and help you realize how very easy it is to make money online.

Here are a few facts and figures to chew over.

One in eight internet users sells something online. Internet traffic data show that between 2008 and 2009, visits to classified-ad websites grew by 80 per cent in a single year. And that's just individual people sitting at home with their computers. Meanwhile, more and more commercial retailers of all kinds are realizing that you have to be online to make money.

Whatever you want, you can buy it somewhere on the internet. A plastic Father Christmas, a ferret harness, stamp collections, bridesmaids dresses, brand new or second-hand items of every kind. Cars, houses and music are all sold online. Farmers are selling their produce direct to the consumer. Craftspeople and artists are finding a market online for their work. People are making money out of their hobbies, their passions, their obsessions, their creative concepts, both physical products and less tangible ideas.

Online services include everything from finding a shoe-repair shop to a stable for your horse, from route finding to the world's best roller coasters, from tips on coping with painful feet to a long-range weather forecast. All those websites that appear to offer intangibles like advice are making money, even if you don't realize it, by creating leads and allowing others to sell through them.

Other people are doing it – if you don't take the plunge you could get left behind. Whether you are an early adopter, who has already dipped a toe in the flow of online commerce, or a total beginner, this book will show you how to create sales and make money online, out of both tangible and intangible stuff.

Too many people are put off because the process seems too complicated or too risky. This book will show you how easy it can be, and what kind of safeguards you will need. It explains what the best-selling things online are, and how to find your own niche.

If you only want to dabble by selling a few unwanted items through a site like eBay, you'll learn the tricks that will make your sale more successful. If you want to take it further, you'll be shown how to:

- set up an online shop;
- organize PayPal;
- test your sales system.

Through case studies of those who are already making money online, you'll learn from the horse's mouth the tips and wrinkles that can make the difference. You'll find out:

- how to sell on Amazon;
- how to sell a house/car;
- how to sell your own photography and other creative products, including games characters on sites like Virtual Life;
- how to monetize your blog;

- how to take money from the gambling websites and come out ahead;
- how to sell leads to other people.

And if you want to start a new business with low overheads, if you're an entrepreneur who wants to try out a new idea, or you already have a small business and want to expand its customer base, there'll be advice that will set you on your way to online success.

So what's stopping you? Reading this book could be the first step to achieving your dreams!

PART I
STARTING UP

CHAPTER 1
GETTING STARTED:
FLEXING YOUR MUSCLES ON eBAY

Everybody has to start somewhere. Top salesmen tell stories of trading marbles or conkers in the school playground; some billionaires began as barrow boys. In the online world, the place where many people begin selling is eBay.

eBay is quite simply the world's biggest marketplace. It is primarily an auction site, but through the *Buy It Now* option also functions as an online shopping mall. It was founded in 1995 by a 28-year-old French-born Iranian computer programmer called Pierre Omidyar, living in San José, California. The story goes – and who knows if it is true or not, but it certainly sums up the spirit of eBay – that the very first item sold on the site was a broken laser pointer, which was auctioned for $14.83. Amazed that the item had raised so much money, Omidyar decided he had better contact the buyer and make sure he understood he had just bought something that didn't work. 'Of course I do,' replied the buyer. 'I'm a collector of broken laser pointers.'

I love this story because for me it sums up what online selling is all about, and it illustrates the first business lesson of this book. Whatever you have to sell, there is somebody somewhere who will buy it. All you have to do is find a way of letting them know what you have for sale, and then agree a price you are both happy with.

In this chapter you will learn:

- how to get started in online selling by offering items for auction on eBay;
- how to present your item;
- how to set a starting price;
- what sellers' and buyers' rating are, and how to use them to make your business more successful;
- how to use *Buy It Now*;
- how to keep your customers coming back for more.

The principles behind these lessons will stand you in good stead not only for trading on eBay, but also for whatever online setting you eventually choose to launch your business.

CASE STUDY

Margaret's online bone china business

I'm going to call her Margaret, because she's a shy lady and didn't want me to use her real name. But she is a real person, and she makes a living out of selling china on the internet. She lives in Staffordshire, UK, but she might just as easily be from Limoges in France, Perth in Australia, or Mumbai in India. eBay is a global marketplace, and Margaret's customers come from all over the world.

Margaret grew up with china, because Staffordshire was once the UK's main centre for pottery manufacture, and indeed one of the world's great centres. Although many of the factories have now disappeared, there is still a huge demand for their wares, both vintage and modern. Margaret's mother worked for most of her life in a pottery factory, and so did Margaret for a while.

'As children, we would be taken round the factories to watch them making the china,' says Margaret. 'I was always fascinated by how the potters took a heap of clay and threw it on the wheel and spun it, until some marvellous shape emerged.'

Having been brought up with china, Margaret loved it, and her cupboard was stacked full of exquisite dinner services she and her mother had collected. But one by one the great names in Staffordshire pottery were closing down, or merging with other brands. Many classic lines had been discontinued. It occurred to Margaret one day, handling a lovely old bone china cup that had become chipped, that there had to be a demand still for these delicate pieces. If you had broken a saucer or cracked a plate from a set made by Doulton or Royal Albert, surely you would want to find a replacement. Besides, there would be collectors of vintage china who would be scouring the internet for pieces to add to their collections.

'Five years ago, when I began trading, it was relatively easy to pick up good pieces of china cheaply at local auctions or junk shops,' says Margaret. 'Around here, the potteries were the biggest employers, and lots of ordinary people had beautiful dinnerware that they had bought at a discount in the factory shops, and kept for special occasions. So I started buying up just a few plates or a bowl at a time, sometimes a whole box at an auction, and advertising it piece by piece on eBay.'

To her delight, Margaret found that she was quickly able to turn a tidy profit. Once she knew there were buyers for these pieces, she could afford to ramp up her business. Her husband began lending a hand, and they have turned the spare bedroom into an office-cum-stockroom, with two computers – one to do the bookkeeping, the other for listing items on eBay and communicating with buyers. A double garage is piled high with more pottery.

'More and more people are doing this kind of thing, so we have to travel further and further to find good china. Some weeks, there might be as many as six or seven auctions we go to. It's quite time consuming, because you must go to the view beforehand, to check that the pottery you're interested in isn't cracked or otherwise damaged. I specialize in Doulton, Wedgwood and Royal Albert – really fine china.'

Who buys it? 'People all over the world. I have a lot of customers in Australia – they can't get fine English china brands like Wedgwood over there, but maybe their families emigrated from the UK, and brought a dinner service with them. My other big seller is Royal Albert's Old Country Rose china – it's one of the prettiest, decorated with pink and red roses. That goes out to Italy all the time – they love it there. I know some of my Italian customers are even buying to resell. Sometimes I think it's a pity that we are sending all our lovely old china abroad, but it's how I make my living. And you know what? I've made lots of friends out of it too. A couple of years ago we went out to Australia to see family, and several of my customers there pressed us to visit them and stay. We've never met any of these people, but they've become friends through trading online.'

The advantage of starting your online selling business in a small way, as Margaret did, is that overheads are low while you are effectively testing the market. eBay is a great place to do this because it is primarily an auction site and you can watch how quickly the bids roll in, to find out how many people are interested in what you have to sell.

Getting started on eBay is very easy. It's worth going on the site to bid for and buy an item or two first, to get the feel of how it works. To use the site to bid or to sell, you have to register, which is simply a matter of giving eBay your details and choosing a username for yourself, which could be anything from your first pet to whatever you see as you look out of the window. By bidding yourself, you'll notice how other sellers describe their goods in the listings, how a good photograph makes an item look far more desirable, and how the site allows interested potential bidders to ask the seller a question, perhaps to clarify the dimensions of the item or its condition. You'll see that most people use PayPal, the payment system owned by eBay, which is designed to safeguard both buyer and seller. It allows the buyer to know that payment has been received before they send out the item, whilst at the same time giving buyers confidence that if the goods don't arrive they have means of recompense.

eBAY RULES AND ETIQUETTE

You'll also realize that selling and buying on eBay is guided by an etiquette as well as a set of rules. Buyers and sellers are expected to trade fairly with one another, and if one party breaches the etiquette, it will be reflected in the online feedback they receive as a buyer or a seller. This is the all-important star-rating system that eBay set up to police people's behaviour on the site, and it usually works very well indeed.

It's a useful principle to grasp before you begin trading online. In a business where you will never meet your customers face to face before the sale, and they are not able to inspect and handle the goods before they buy, you have to be able to fill them with confidence that you are not out to con them. Many people are still suspicious of buying online, and reputation is your best, indeed your *only*, means of persuading people to trust you and your wares.

eBay's system works well because it not only reflects what other people think of you after they have dealt with you, it also measures how 'experienced' a trader you are. Buyers and sellers are awarded different-coloured stars depending on how many transactions they have carried out. You'll find that other buyers and sellers will ask you to leave honest feedback after trading, because this can enhance their reputation, and make other people happier to buy from them or accept their bids in the future. Of course, it is not an entirely foolproof system, but although rogue traders may try to get away with rip-offs by constantly changing user names, they will then have denied themselves the advantage of a long track record of trading under a particular name.

Buyers often prefer to deal with established sellers rather than novices. But reputation works both ways. When you set up your eBay listing, you could choose only to accept bids from buyers who have bought before and have a good reputation. (Remember, however, this could be counter-productive as it will cut down the pool of people who are likely to bid for your item – everybody has to go through the stage of being a novice buyer!)

RESERVES AND STARTING PRICES

The rules are simple. Once you have advertised an item on eBay, and accepted bids, you cannot withdraw it from sale just because it has not achieved as high a price as you hoped. If the reserve or starting price has been reached, the item has to go to the highest bidder. It can only be with-drawn if the item fails to reach your starting price. It is tempt-ing to set the starting price very low, either to attract opening bids or for the simple reason that the lowest starting price allows you to advertise your item for sale free of charge. But you may be disappointed if the item only makes the reserve or a little above it. Setting your starting price too low to avoid paying charges is a false economy. Instead, pick the lowest price you would be happy receiving!

eBay also offers you the option of choosing to list the item at a *Buy It Now* price. This enables buyers to pre-empt the auction and buy at a price considerably above the reserve. 'If someone asks me to sell at a *Buy It Now*, I'll refuse 99.9 per cent of the time,' says Margaret. 'To me eBay is an auction site, and that's its appeal.' However, if no one else has yet bid for the item, and you have received a query from a possible buyer asking you to consider *Buy It Now*, you might want to settle on a mutually agreeable price and close the auction. You will not be allowed to do this, though, if there is a 'best bid' already on the table.

Buyers have to remember that the terms and condi-tions of buying in an auction are very different from what they might be used to when buying from a shop. There is no cooling-off period or right of return, unless an item is not as described. You cannot bid frivolously and wriggle out of buying the item just because you have changed your mind. Once you bid, as at any auction, you enter into a contract to buy should yours be the winning bid. Nor can you change your mind and send the item back just because you don't like it. The only grounds for rejecting an item are either that it has been damaged in transit or that it is not as described by the seller. This even applies to clothes and shoes that don't fit. Buyer beware! But as we'll see, the seller has to be careful too.

PayPal

Transactions are policed by PayPal's dispute system, which is another reason why it is sensible and safer for buyer and seller to use PayPal rather than a cheque in the post or cash. If either buyer or seller feels they have cause to complain about the transaction, and they are unable to settle the matter amicably between them, they must contact PayPal and take out a dispute. This safeguards a buyer if an item has been falsely described – buyers have 45 days from the date of payment to initiate a dispute – but it also safeguards sellers against buyers who do not pay up within the set period. In such cases, the seller is allowed to re-advertise the item on eBay free of charge. Many disputes arise because the buyer or the seller does not fully understand the rules of trading on an auction site – so make sure you do!

Sellers often complain that PayPal finds more often in favour of the buyer than the seller, and is therefore biased. But remember the golden principle that successful selling online is all about reputation. Long before the internet was thought of, reputable traders used to operate on the principle that the customer is always right, and it is important to maintain your buyers' confidence that they will always be treated fairly, even if occasionally it means giving way to a troublesome customer whose case is weak. In the end, you want customers to keep coming back!

Another useful part of eBay's site is the online help section where new sellers pose questions to be answered by more experienced traders. It will open your eyes to some of the problems that can arise – though you shouldn't let yourself be put off! The Q&A forums are specifically designed for people who have run into difficulties, whereas most transactions on eBay run remarkably smoothly.

Once you are ready to start selling, start simply as Margaret did with just one or two items until you have the hang of it. Everything you need to know is explained in detail on eBay's help pages, including charges for selling, and how to initiate disputes, but it is still worth running through the basics here.

YOUR LISTING OR ONLINE ADVERT

Photographing your item

The purpose of this is to make the item look as attractive as possible to the buyer, so it is worth taking time to get it right. First, you need a good photograph of the item. Don't just rely on a snatched snap using your mobile phone – use a decent digital camera and set up the item so that it is shown at its best. As any professional photographer will tell you, getting the lighting right is vital. Turn on as much light as you can in the room – bring extra lamps in if necessary, and direct them at the object you are photographing. There will always be more light out of doors, especially on a sunny day, so sometimes you might want to take the item outside to get the best shot. But remember that you don't want to give people the impression the item is being kept outside, if it is something that could be damaged! It's ideal to take a picture of the item in the kind of setting where it would be used. Plan ahead, so if you are hoping to sell something like an unwanted bath or built-in cooker, photograph it before you take it out of the bathroom or kitchen.

Describing your item

Margaret is careful always to describe the item she is selling as exactly as possible – and that means being honest about any flaws or defects. Nobody expects second-hand items to be as perfect as those that are new, but buyers will reject items that are damaged if you have not mentioned that in your description. Some sellers safeguard themselves further by photographing the flaw. But the golden rule is *never* to describe an item as in 'good condition' unless it demonstrably is. Indeed it is much safer not to make vague claims about its condition. Instead, tell people more concrete things like how old it is, how much use it has had, and where the minor flaws are. Your honesty will pay in the long run – when you don't have to refund irate buyers!

Setting the price at the right level is the next step. You need to attract buyers, so make the reserve price realistically low. Look at other listings for similar items and see how the bidding goes for those before you settle on a price.

'It's really trial and error,' explains Margaret. 'I'll list things as cheaply as I can, but I've made mistakes, of course, and lost money by listing things *too* cheaply. You learn from that and you don't make the same error twice. If an item doesn't sell at all, I will give it a second go, re-advertising a few weeks later, perhaps adjusting the starting price. Sometimes I've bought a whole box of china from an auction and not one piece has sold – in which case I put it back in a local auction and hope someone else has better luck! But it's swings and roundabouts – I'm here to sell and not to hoard, so I need to keep stock moving.'

eBay fees and costs

The charges you pay for selling on eBay depend upon various factors, like the format you choose for your ad and the reserve price you are advertising the item at. You will also pay an additional percentage for using PayPal, so don't forget to factor all these costs into the price you set.

Basically when you create a listing for your item on eBay, you will be charged an **insertion** fee which depends on the starting price. There are **listing upgrade** fees which allow you to add extra pictures or special headings to your ad. When you sell, you are charged a **final value** fee depending on the price you sell for.

You must also work out postage and delivery charges, as buyers want to know these costs up front. Don't guesstimate – weigh and measure the item, work out how much bubble wrap and packing materials you will need, and get quotes from the Post Office or delivery companies. If you make a guess and there is a shortfall, you will be the one who has to pay. But if you are advertising a very large item, or a particularly delicate one, you may want to stipulate that the buyer has to collect it from you instead.

You can change the wording of your ad or add photographs even after the auction has begun. You can even lower the reserve price, though you will still have to pay eBay the charges for your original starting price. This is useful if the item is not attracting many bids. But remember too that sometimes buyers wait until the last moment before bidding, in the hope you might drop your reserve.

DELIVERY

Successful eBay sellers deliver – in every sense of the word. What happens after the auction is just as important as the way you prepare for it.

Once you have received notification from PayPal that payment has been received, you should post the item as soon as possible, and certainly within seven days (unless the buyer is going to collect it, in which case you should make arrangements for this).

Whatever carrier you use, make sure you retain online trackable proof of delivery. This will help protect you in the event of a dispute. 'Things do go missing in the post,' says Margaret. 'The customer expects you to know where everything is every step of the way, so you need to be able to get onto the carrier and find out what has happened to the item.'

And don't skimp on packaging! 'With pottery, or anything breakable, you have to pack it really, really well. I double box all the china I sell, by bubble wrapping it, boxing it, bubble wrapping it again and then boxing it again. It's worth it to get the product there in one piece.'

Most sales on eBay go through without any problems. But in the event of an issue arising between buyer and seller, act immediately. Don't delay and hope the problem will go away – it won't! Again there are full details on the eBay help pages about how to initiate and respond to disputes, but there are two key rules to remember:

- First, it is always better, if you can, to resolve things amicably between you and the buyer before it reaches official dispute status, in order to maintain your reputation as a good and fair seller.

- Second, if it does escalate to a dispute, respond promptly to any queries from eBay or PayPal before the deadlines, as all disputes have to be resolved within a set period, usually within ten days of the customer initiating the complaint.

But perhaps the most useful lesson to remember is Margaret's guiding principle: 'It doesn't have to make us a fortune,' she says. 'We do make a profit, but really it's just that I love china, and we love selling it. That's the key to success, isn't it? Loving what you do. If you don't enjoy it, you shouldn't be doing it.'

TOP TIPS

 Don't be afraid of starting small. It's the best way to test the market!

 Photograph your item in the best possible light, and take time to choose a good picture.

 Describe it accurately.

 Make sure you set your starting (reserve) price low enough to be attractive to buyers...

 ...but high enough to satisfy you!

 Don't forget to calculate postage and packing charges in advance.

 Make sure you deliver – in every sense of the word!

 Wrap the item well before dispatching, to minimize breakages.

 Act quickly to resolve any problems.

 Sell what you love and love what you sell.

QUESTION

Can I sell more than one thing in the same listing?

Technically yes – so long as they are being sold as a set. What you cannot do is take separate offers for them. So you could, for instance, sell a washbasin and its taps via the same ad, or a vacuum cleaner along with a set of bags, but they couldn't be split, and would have to be sold to the same person in one single transaction.

ACTIVITY

Log onto eBay and bid for and buy an item, to get the feel of how it works. To use the site to bid or to sell, you have to register, which is simply a matter of giving eBay your details and choosing a username. The purpose of this activity is to find out how other sellers describe their goods in the listings, how a good photograph makes an item look far more desirable, and how the site allows interested potential bidders to ask the seller questions. Understanding your customer is key to selling, and so becoming a customer yourself is a good starting point.

CHAPTER 2
SELLING VIA YOUR OWN ONLINE SHOP

The beauty of selling online is that there are so many levels at which you can choose to pitch your business. You could be satisfied, as Margaret was in the previous chapter, with a small-scale operation selling entirely through eBay listings, and still make a comfortable living. Or you could move on to the next stage, and grow your business by setting up your own online shop.

Nervous of taking the plunge? Setting up your own website to sell online can feel like a major commitment. There are so many new responsibilities: processing payments, handling confidential data, security. But again, you can take it step by step. Just as there are many different levels of High Street selling, from Saturday market stallholder to globally branded superstore, so there are many different kinds of online shop. Of course, there will be a small initial outlay, for the design and maintenance of your website, but think of it as the rental for your market stall! Eventually you might move up to dominate your chosen market, or expand into other fields to build the equivalent of an online Marks and Spencer or Walmart – but that's for the future.

You have probably already taken the first step of deciding what kind of product you will sell. Now you have to take just one small step more to lay the foundations of your own online enterprise.

In this chapter you will learn:

- the simplest form of individual online shop to set up;
- how the payment process works;
- what to consider when choosing your shopping cart software;
- the five stages of building an e-commerce website;
- whether it is better to employ your own designer to create a unique website for you;
- or whether it could be easier to buy an 'off-the-peg' e-commerce solution.

CASE STUDY

Chris Seagon's herb farm

Chris Seagon has been cultivating herbs and selling them for 25 years. It's not the easiest business to make a living in, especially during a recession, but Laurel Farm Herbs is one of the leading online retailers of herbs in the UK. Chris takes a pride in what he does, and grows herbs at his East Anglia nursery according to best 'green' practice, in peat-free compost, without artificial heating and without chemicals.

Ten years ago, Chris took the decision to begin selling his herbs online. 'It was a complete and utter flop the first year', he admits. 'We set up on 1 April, and people thought it was a joke. No one believed I was serious – especially as one of the newspaper ads we bought failed to print our web address or telephone number! But I was absolutely committed, and selling online eventually helped us become one of the big three herb growers in the UK.'

His business sends live herb plants all over the country. He offers nine different kinds of basil and 33 different varieties of thyme!

His first website was built by a web designer recommended by a friend of a friend. 'He had a site with a shopping cart in his portfolio, and there was a grant available at the time,' says Chris. 'So I went for it. I did my best to screw him down hard on price, but somehow there turned out to be a lot more work in it than either of us had envisaged, and I found myself being stretched and stretched on cost. In the end that relationship didn't work out. I'm onto my third web designer now, who is very reasonable and works quickly.'

Chris is the first to admit he isn't a technical genius as far as computers go. 'I don't understand the technical side at all – I know how to find stuff and that's about it. So if there are problems or something I want changed on the site, I just e-mail the designer and he sorts it, usually within 24 hours.'

Chris's site is simple and effective. A colourful home page tells the customer about the business. The stand-out colour is green, and there are well-chosen photos of lush and healthy herb plants. On the navigation bar you can click on a straight-forward and self-explanatory row of buttons that take you to different pages:

- *Ordering Herbs* is a page that explains the process.

- *Order Online* takes you to the online catalogue, illustrated with pictures of each different variety of herb. It's easy to navigate around the catalogue, as a list of the different types appears vertically at the side of the page, so you can jump quickly from angelica to woodruff, and anything in between.

- The catalogue is also available for download as a PDF document.

- Other pages tell you how and when to visit Laurel Farm, and which fairs and markets they are appearing at.

- There is an all-important page of customers' feedback, to give potential buyers confidence in the company's delivery process and the quality of their products.

- *Links* take browsers to other websites that contain articles about cooking with herbs or planning a herb garden.

- There's even a page for latest news, which at the time of writing shows a picture of the company's latest security guard, Sandy the rescue puppy.

This is typical of Chris's approach to the business, which is to make online ordering as customer friendly and as personal as he can. Although you can order from the site through the usual 'shopping basket' and 'checkout', he does not actually take payment online. Instead, customers' orders reach him by e-mail and he then phones them up personally to take payment by credit card, or they can post him a personal cheque. It's a straightforward system that works for him, saving the cost of transacting through a secure server and a payment gateway. It also works well for his customers.

'A lot of people still don't entirely trust online commerce and they prefer that personal touch – they enjoy chatting to the boss of the business on the phone,' he says. 'Adding the capacity to take payment online can cost a lot more, because there are rules and regulations about setting up secure servers and so on. I'd have to look for a specialist in that side of things if I wanted to take the website down that road, and I'm happier keeping it friendly and personal.'

Chris's approach strikes a good balance at a point where e-commerce is still in its developmental stages. He understands his customers well – the kind of consumers who buy herb plants are frequently more mature people not yet entirely comfortable with buying online. Customer attitudes to payment systems should be taken into account when planning an online shop.

It also illustrates how you need not have every technological bell and whistle on your site to be successful. A shopping basket and a checkout are useful to take the order, but it is by no means necessary to go to the expense of setting up an online payment process to start selling online.

PLANNING FOR THE SIMPLEST ONLINE SHOP

Even at entry level, though, you need a website that is attractive and professional like Chris's, and unless you are very confident in your abilities, it is sensible to pay someone else to do the basic design for you.

Designing your website

Find a web designer you trust, preferably one recommended by someone else. There are plenty of eager young designers out there bursting with splendid ideas, but make sure that yours also has the capacity to follow through and will not lose enthusiasm before the project is completed! Be wary of the 'something for nothing' offer. Almost everybody has a cousin or a nephew or a friend who is clever with computers. Whether that person can be relied on to finish the job, and to build you a site that looks professional and works efficiently in an increasingly professionalized market, is another matter. Customers soon become fed up with a site they can't easily navigate to find what they are looking for.

Before you settle on a particular style and structure for the site, take time to look around at what the competition are doing online. Find out how other people are selling, what pages they put on their websites, how easy it is to navigate their catalogue. In other words, act like a consumer. By visiting other sites you will soon pick up what are the common mistakes to avoid. Also take a good look at what their minimum orders are, and what they charge for carriage. Chris, for instance, insists on minimum orders of 12 herb plants, and his carriage fee is realistic, because it is vital with a product like a living plant to make sure it is packed securely and handled well in transit so that it arrives in a healthy condition.

Before you talk to the designer, develop ideas of your own about the kind of image you want to project for your business. The look of the site says as much about your brand as the content, and the designer needs your input to help them build the right site. What background colours best showcase your products?

Start to assemble material that could be used to illustrate your inventory: good pictures, clear descriptions of each product.

Take time to think about the associated content you want on the site to complement the product range. News of events you will be involved with or fairs where you will be exhibiting? Links to other content elsewhere on the web that helps to whet your customers' appetite for the products? You may want to write about the background of your enterprise; introduce customers to your staff; and generally to humanize the business.

DO YOUR RESEARCH

Indeed, the design of the site isn't the only aspect of your fledgling enterprise to plan. It's essential, as in any business venture, to have done thorough market research and to project costings before you jump in.

Chris points out that it can be a lot more difficult than you realize to make a profit on some products. 'I would say to anyone, 'What do you want to work for – pennies or pounds?' A chap I know thought he'd make a killing on herbs. He'd worked out seed was cheap, and he could fit 10,000 9-centimetre pots into his glasshouse. He assumed that would give him a really good living. But it takes up to two years to produce a strong plant from seed, and it's not a nine-to-five job – plants need care seven days a week. In the end he realized he'd have to produce *30,000* pots a year to make any profit at all.'

So work out the viability of your online selling proposition well before you start. You may not necessarily expect to clear a profit in this first year or two, but a business that goes on making you pennies isn't a business at all; it's a hobby!

SHOPPING CARTS, CHECKOUT AND PAYMENT

As Chris's example illustrates, you don't have to offer online payment via the site to be successful. But as e-commerce grows, it will become more and more standard practice that people not only order but also pay online.

Not only do your customers want to be certain their money is safe when they carry out internet transactions, but the business of online payment has become increasingly the subject of regulation. Your customers' payments should be taken via a secure server, with the help of a payment gateway such as PayPal or one of the many other companies who offer such a service to online businesses.

The mechanics of online payment

When your customer clicks the *Pay* button on the site, their money goes through a payment gateway. PayPal, owned by eBay but available to any website, is known internationally, but there are also, for example, Secure Trading, Sage Pay, NETBANX, Worldpay and others. The gateway company then settles the fund to an acquirer, which will be a merchant service – in the UK it might be Lloyds TSB, Cardnet or Barclaycard, in Ireland most probably Elavon – and so the money is processed and reaches your account.

These acquirers will settle funds to banks in other countries in the appropriate currency, so if your business is in Canada but your customer wishes to pay in pounds sterling, the payment will be converted for you into Canadian dollars – or vice versa. (Of course, if you do a lot of business in a particular country, you might decide to open a bank account there to avoid currency transfer fees.)

Which gateway you choose to handle your shop's payments might depend on the percentage of the transaction they charge. You might get better rates from some providers, but decide nonetheless to go with a better-known name because it will be more appealing to your customers. But it is worth shopping around to find the best deal on your shopping cart.

WEBSITE SECURITY

Customers need reassurance that their personal details will be safe when they entrust them to the site. Online sellers have to buy security certificates for their domains – this is where a small padlock appears at the bottom of the screen, or the bar shows a different colour, depending on the customer's browser, indicating that they are in a secure area.

But there are other questions to consider. Is the site infrastructure set up in a way to prevent hacking attacks, where someone fakes an interaction with a website to steal data from it?

Again these are questions you should consider carefully before settling on any e-commerce software. This is not an area for amateurs to try creating home-made solutions. Get it wrong, and it may have dire repercussions for your business!

If your head is already starting to spin with the sheer technicality of it, don't worry. Basically, there are **two different approaches** to setting up a payment process for an online shop. Both can work well, and neither need cost the earth. The approach you take may depend on whether or not you already have a website set up for your business.

Approach One: Going it alone (with a bit of help)

If you already have a website, and you want to keep it much as it is, your feet are on the do-it-yourself path. Maybe you have a business that has a presence online to advertise your existence, but now you want to start selling your products via the internet too. Or perhaps, like Chris, you are already selling successfully online but so far have only taken payment over the phone or by post. With the help of the web designer, you add to your site a shopping cart and the capacity to pay at checkout by creating a relationship with a gateway. This need not be expensive: often the company with whom you have registered your domain name will offer a secure shopping cart facility for only a small monthly subscription. PayPal itself allows you to add a shopping cart for free (though of course it charges you for the transactions you make via it).

The advantages of this approach are that it can be cheap and relatively easy. You have the freedom to design exactly the website you want or adapt an existing one. For many small businesses it will be the ideal solution.

But there are also some drawbacks. Cheap shopping cart software may have limited flexibility. It may tie you in to a server that demands an additional fee for hosting, and thus not be as cheap as it seemed.

You also have to consider what kind of support you will have from your service provider. Will you have to pay for support? And how reliably will the provider keep your shop up and running online? Customers quickly tire of a site that keeps crashing or has apparently disappeared after they Google it.

Approach Two: Buying an e-commerce package deal

Rather than go to the trouble of designing your website and then bolting on a shopping cart, you could instead head straight for one of the many specialist e-commerce suppliers that set up and maintain the website for you, and take much of the hassle and worry out of the process. In return, they take either a monthly subscription or a share of the revenue from your site.

'At the lower end of this model you find examples like the eBay shop,' says Chris Rodgers, whose company supplies e-commerce solutions to both large and small online businesses. 'People who have been selling for a while through the listings on eBay might decide to move up eventually to an eBay shop. For a monthly subscription, they will be supplied with templates to design a shop front that displays all the items they sell, as well as marketing and reporting tools and telephone support. All the tricky stuff has been done for them. Companies like ours provide a broadly similar service, though we offer a more sophisticated range of solutions, from basic to bespoke.'

There are a number of similar companies in the field that can be found by Googling 'e-commerce software'. Usually they provide various levels of service, from cheap and cheerful entry level to online megastore.

'For example, we have a product at the lower end called Transact,' says Chris Rodgers. 'We take a revenue share, and you pay nothing until you sell, so there is no financial risk. Your only potential loss is the time you spend creating the website.'

The package bypasses the need to employ your own website designer. 'Once you've signed up for it online, you receive details via e-mail that give you access to an administration system. This then guides you through the five main steps to create your website: it's a form-filling process that isn't complicated at all. First you select a design from a range of templates, then you add products with descriptions, pictures and prices. Next, static content is added, before the final two stages: setting up payments and then setting up shipping.'

These are of course the same steps you would follow to create any selling website. Throughout the process the online seller is offered a number of alternatives. There may be a choice of payment gateways, or the e-commerce provider will present you with several carriage options.

It's worth shopping around to find a provider that offers the right kind of shippers to suit your product. Chris Seagon, with living plants to send out, needs a particular kind of courier he can rely on to deliver quickly and not distress the product. Other sellers may prefer slower, cheaper carriers, but with an option for customers to upgrade to next-day delivery. (Doing the delivery yourself is, in a very few localized instances, a possibility, but usually employing a carrier is a far more cost-effective solution. Rather than driving the length and breadth of the country, you'd be better employed running your business and processing the orders.)

Essentially the e-commerce software supplier is offering a one-stop solution, from website design via templates to shopping cart, payment gateway and shippers. They take on the responsibility of hosting your site, and because their whole business is geared to efficient online commerce they provide solid support and high site availability, so the risk of your online shop being unavailable to customers is diminished. Updates and patches to the software are all taken care of for you.

Low-end packages offer a range of templates to set up the site. Higher-end products allow you to upload bespoke design tools or to bring your own designers into the process.

When choosing your e-commerce software provider, you also need to think about how you will receive information from your website, in order to process orders or deal with complaints. Will you simply view it on the website and process it online? Or will you download to an Excel spreadsheet and go through it every evening? Do you want to integrate the ordering process into Sage or similar software that makes your accounting easier at the end of each month? Other tools such as Google Analytics are available to check how well the site is working for you. There should also be flexibility to alter the content and structure after you are up and running.

'With the best will in the world, an online seller can get it wrong in the early days,' says Chris. 'We make it easy for you to add product content to the website – it's a simple form-filling exercise. But you have to come up with the content in the first place, and that's the hard part: creating the content to explain the product and make it attractive to the customer.'

Categorizing your items

Then there is the question of how to categorize items, especially if you are a kind of online department store selling many different ranges and types of product. 'For instance, how do you categorize a bathmat?' asks Chris. 'Does it appear under a section called Textiles or Linens? Does it go in with the towels or with floor coverings? You maybe need to have a section called Bathroom Accessories. But there are infinite degrees of refining so that customers can easily find what they want. All these things need thinking about. Bear in mind that it won't be *you* buying from the site, with all your knowledge of the products – real customers may think in a different way. In the light of experience and customer feedback, you may need to change the way your catalogue is set up. So make sure you choose a software platform with the flexibility to make changes throughout the life of the site.'

Whatever your level of technical competence, there will always be someone who can help you with setting up an online shop. Assistance in building an e-commerce website and keeping it running smoothly need not cost a lot. There is no need to reinvent the wheel – although e-commerce is still developing, plenty of people have gone before you, and you can profit from their experience and learn by their mistakes!

TOP TIPS

- Study your competitors' sites to discover what works and what doesn't.

- Put time and thought into the look and the content of the site.

- Prepare good pictures and clear, compelling copy that explains your product and makes it attractive to buyers.

- Look for ways of personalizing and humanizing your business via the website.

- Before settling on a shopping cart, decide which route you would prefer: an off-the-peg e-commerce solution or a more bespoke site?

- If the latter, employ the best and most reliable designer you can afford; this is not the area to economize.

- Always check what kind of ongoing support you will get from your provider.

- Plan carefully how your customer will browse the catalogue to find what they are looking for.

- Use analytics tools to assess how well your site is performing for you.

- Be prepared to alter the structure of your site in the light of customer feedback.

QUESTION

I'm leaning towards buying an off-the peg e-commerce solution for cost reasons – but might I regret it if my business takes off? Would I have to upgrade to a bigger server and start all over again?

Not necessarily. Many e-commerce software suppliers have taken such an eventuality into account. They share their platform and their infrastructure across all their customers and have therefore a large enough capacity to deal with whatever you throw at them. But you are right to have taken the possibility into account, and it's certainly a question you should put directly to any supplier before committing yourself.

ACTIVITY

Research your business before you start selling – who is selling similar products and how much do they charge? It makes sense to choose a product for which you are the expert, and if you start a business in something that is also your hobby or passion, you'll have fun as well as make money.

CHAPTER 3
TESTING YOUR SALES SYSTEM

So now you've taken the big step and set yourself up as a committed online seller. Maybe your 'shop window' is through an online marketplace like eBay or Amazon, or you have taken the step of building your own sales website. Either way, you're just raring to go and make money!

But hold on. Before you start selling, there's something important you *must* do. You need to test your sales system.

Don't be impatient. If you don't get checkout and delivery right, you run the risk of alienating customers. They will not only refuse to buy again from you, but might well also tell all their friends about the bad experience they had. Sales experts used to say that a dissatisfied customer will tell a minimum of seven other people – that's *eight* potential customers you could lose through a single mistake. If you go on making mistakes ... well, do the maths!

In this chapter you will learn:

- the four key steps to test in your sales system;
- how to get customers to trust you;
- the way to set up and test a system for delivery;

- common pitfalls to avoid;
- how to handle complaints and still hold on to your customers!

CASE STUDY

Phil Moolman

Phil Moolman's online selling business almost died before it had a chance to grow.

Phil, from Natal, South Africa, has always been fascinated by guitars. 'Can't play 'em,' he says. 'But I love them. The shapes and the surfaces are so seductive. When you see a white maple-necked Fender Strat like the one Jimi Hendrix used to play, or a copy of the Red Special that Brian May's father made him – well, you just have to have it. I've been collecting guitars since I was in my 20s. Trouble is, you reach the point you've run out of room.'

Matters came to a head when the guitars spilled out of Phil's den and his wife Ruby found him hanging a row of them along the side of the stairs. 'I thought it was a pretty cool way of decorating,' he says. 'Not Ruby. Basically, she gave me an ultimatum – either the guitars went or she did. I talked her down from that, but in the interests of harmony I had to agree that the guitars stayed in my den, and if I wanted to buy a new one, I'd have to sell one of the others.'

Phil advertised a guitar on eBay and was amazed when bids rolled in and he made three times his starting price. Before long he was trading in guitars and guitar parts on a regular basis, dispatching to buyers as far away as the United States and Japan. 'I liked repairing guitars, and often you'd find you were left with a spare pick-up or whatever, and you could make a few rand out of that too.'

But then the problems started. 'Some guy in Durban e-mailed me and complained the Flying V he'd bought had never arrived. I thought he was trying it on – I knew I'd sent it. Next thing I know, he's taken out a dispute through PayPal, they find in his favour, and I get bad feedback on my seller rating.'

Only a couple of weeks later, Phil had another complaint from a customer about non-delivery. This time, the guitar was eventually returned by the carrier, and luckily Ruby happened to be around when Phil was unpacking it.

'Look, you got the customer's name wrong,' she said. 'This label says the guitar's for Rupert Goulding, not Robert Golding. You're copying down addresses incorrectly.' Sharp-eyed Ruby had spotted the flaw in Phil's sales system. He was transcribing the customer's names and addresses by hand onto the postage labels and, being mildly dyslexic, often making a mistake. Most of the time the parcels still got through, but every so often someone would be out, and the neighbour the postman tried to leave the package with didn't recognize the name, or the address itself would be so wildly wrong the parcels were sometimes lost for months in the postal system.

'You don't have to transcribe them,' Ruby pointed out. 'It's easy enough to copy and paste. Or why don't you let me handle the delivery paperwork for you?'

Ruby took over and organized the way the sales were handled. The complaints stopped, their online seller ratings soared, and Phil's hobby started to turn a profit.

'It never even occurred to me I could be making mistakes,' Phil admits. 'Or that even one or two errors could so quickly poison your relationship with customers. Thank God for Ruby.'

Testing your sales system is vital, to avoid making simple mistakes like Phil's.

'The idea is to find the problems and fix them *before* the customers see them,' says Tom Norris, Director of Consulting at Acutest, who specializes in testing systems and processes for many well-known companies. 'Then your customers are going to be happy because they will never know there was a problem in the first place. Remember, when you never meet your customers face to face, your reputation is the only thing you have to help you sell.'

There are four key elements to your sales system that you should test:

- The way you **describe** the goods – is it clear and accurate?

- The way the goods are **paid for** – is it fail-safe?

- The system you use for **delivery** – will the experience be hassle-free for the customer?

- How you handle **complaints and refunds** – have you worked out a consistent policy that will leave your customer thinking they have been dealt with fairly in the event of a mistake?

It doesn't matter whether you are a hobby seller, offloading a few items on eBay, or an entrepreneur planning to grow an online retail empire. Happy customers mean repeat sales. Unhappy customers could kill off your business.

The whole point of sales system testing is to start thinking like a customer. Ask yourself whether everything will run as smoothly as you would want if you were buying? Where are the snags and niggles? What can you do to make the customer's experience less irritating and more satisfying?

'There are three things that matter in testing,' says Tom Norris. 'One is the ease of the transaction. If the customer experience is silky smooth, they'll come back for more. The second is finding problems early, before your customers do. We call that a "fail fast". It sounds nutty, but the faster you fail the test, the better: the sooner you find the problem and solve it. The third is to think through the likelihood of things going wrong and the impact that the problem will have on the customer (so a fault on your site stopping someone from buying might annoy, but failing to deliver something they have purchased has a much greater impact on how a buyer is feeling). How can I avoid annoying my customer, and how can I make them happy again if I do?'

DESCRIBING THE GOODS

Your description is what secures a sale (or not) in the first place. You need to be clear in the way you describe goods, and it is vital to be accurate. If you get the dimensions wrong, or forget, accidentally or on purpose, to mention a flaw, you will annoy customers who buy in good faith and find the item isn't as they expected. Then you will have to refund their money and everyone's time will have been wasted.

So measure accurately, and make it clear whether measurements are in metric or in imperial, and in what units – millimetres or centimetres, inches or feet. If the item is second-hand or a factory second, make it clear if there are flaws, and ideally photograph them. If you are selling clothing, and the sizing comes up smaller than average – if for instance, the labels says women's size 16, but it really only fits a 14, say so. Make it clear whether sizing is European or US. Remember that when a customer makes an assumption, if this assumption turns out to be wrong they will think that you have described the goods inaccurately. If they look and they are not sure, they probably won't buy.

When you have written your online description of what you have for sale, ask a friend to check it for you – ideally one who is good at spelling! Many buyers are put off by an ad that is poorly spelt or lacks proper punctuation. The way the online copy is written will be read by customers as saying something about you as a seller. A description that is hastily written and badly spelt suggests that the seller might be sloppy and offhand in the way they dispatch the goods. Get your friend to look over the item you are selling and tell you, honestly, whether they think it matches your description, and if they can see flaws you missed.

If you haven't described the item clearly, people won't buy from you – they'll look elsewhere. Given a choice between these two ads on eBay, which would you buy?

2nd hand bath big not to deep wite with taps buyer colects London area

Or:

White bath for sale, made of double-layer steel, manufacturer is Bette. Dimensions: 1700 × 700 mm, shallow model easy to get into for older or less mobile person, suitable for showering as well as bathing. Two tap holes, chrome waste and Victorian-style taps included. Reason for sale: we are doing up our bathroom and although this bath is only three years old we have decided to replace it as it doesn't match the look we're going for. There is a small chip on the edge of the bath (see photograph). Buyer to collect from Reigate, Surrey.

Remember, people buying online are often worried about how the safe the transaction is and whether they can trust the seller. They imagine the internet is full of conmen and rip-offs. When the item arrives, especially if they have secured it for a bargain price, they will look it over very carefully indeed, and it is important not to give them an excuse to reject the goods.

If you have your own website and sell a range of goods, make sure it is easy for your customers to find what they want. Get your friends to go to your site and search for different products – you want honest feedback and you must take notice of what it says.

TESTING CHECKOUT

For casual sellers on eBay and similar sites, you will find that the site itself helps you set up a simple secure payment system, often through PayPal, that will alert you when payment has gone through so you can release the goods, and that will handle disputes between buyer and seller when they arise. This kind of system is much safer than relying on cheques through the post or cash on collection, and it inspires confidence in the buyer that they can trade safely with you without being ripped off.

When you have your own website, there are a variety of payment systems you can choose. Whichever you go for, make sure you test the checkout process, over and over again! This is especially important if you sometimes allow customers to apply special-offer codes. Nothing is more frustrating for a buyer than to see the total adding up wrongly, and they will pull out immediately if this happens. It is just as counterproductive to have a checkout system that doesn't clearly itemize what is being bought and how much each item costs. The customer will not go ahead if they feel the payment process is not completely transparent.

You don't need to employ a specialist company to do the testing for you, though bigger firms often find it useful to call in experts. Persuade one of your friends to act as a 'secret shopper' and order something from you. You can always give them the money to do so provided they give the item back!

'You want to be absolutely sure that everything is going to work in a predictable, organized, efficient way,' says Tom Norris. 'It isn't necessarily about the technology: it's about the way you and other people interact with the technology.'

Committed online sellers who have built their own sales website might want to consider how different browsers will work with their system. A sale might proceed smoothly to checkout with Microsoft Windows and Internet Explorer, for instance, but founder with Firefox or with someone using an Apple Mac. 'It's as if you're at the supermarket and someone tips your trolley over,' says Tom. 'You were standing at the checkout and the store manager leads you back to the front door and tells you to start over again. Most people would walk out at that point and never return.'

Do you also want your site to work beautifully on an iPhone or a Blackberry or other smartphone? As technology moves on, keep testing and don't get left behind.

DELIVERING THE GOODS

'Most sales problems come about not through faulty technology but through simple human error,' says Tom Norris. 'Especially when it comes to delivery.'

Set up an organized system so you won't make a mistake transcribing the name or the address, like Phil did, or, if you are handling a lot of sales, so you won't put the goods in the wrong envelope! Everything has to work efficiently, and the best way of making sure is to develop a routine that you *never* change.

COMMON ERRORS

It's important to stick to your word. If you say you'll send it out first-class delivery but actually dispatch it by a slower method such as parcel post and it takes two weeks to arrive, it could have disastrous repercussions. Customer confidence in online selling is created by feedback, and unless you quickly build up and maintain those all-important star ratings, people will be reluctant to buy from you.

If you are sending a package to someone at a big company, make sure the individual's name and department are on the label, or the package could languish for weeks in the post room. It might be their internal system at fault, but *you* will be the one to get the blame!

'Another common error is to muddle up the paperwork,' says Tom Norris. 'One client I worked with put the wrong invoice in the wrong package. As a result, one of their most profitable customers discovered that another customer was getting a bigger discount. They were furious and demanded that prices were slashed for them too. My client lost thousands as a result of that simple slip.'

Tom advises having someone walk through the dispatch process with you, to see if they can spot problems you might have missed. Once you reach a level of selling dozens of items a week, persuade your friends to act as secret shoppers and report back on their experience. They may open your eyes to problems you had no idea of – deliveries left by the carrier on doorsteps, becoming soaked in the rain or stolen!

One of the commonest errors is to dispatch a small item in packaging that is too big to fit through the letterbox. If the customer is out, they may end up with the irritation of having to make a trip to the post office or the carrier's depot to collect it. You could make their experience so much happier just by changing the envelope size!

HANDLING COMPLAINTS AND REFUNDS

Never forget the old saying that the customer is always right. Anyone who has sold online can tell you hair-curling stories about buyers from hell who were very much in the wrong – but nevertheless, the online process has to be weighted in their favour, for without customer confidence you cannot successfully sell. Just one bad review can put customers off.

So you must plan a system for dealing with complaints and refunds.

'Be clear about your policy,' says Tom Norris. 'Say whether goods are being sold on a try-before-you-buy basis or not. If you are selling clothes or shoes, people want to know beforehand that if it doesn't fit, they can send the item back.'

You will also have to think of a way of protecting returns while they are on their way back to you. 'The moment customers put the return in the post box, they assume it's back with you,' says Tom. 'You need a bulletproof way of making sure they understand they should obtain proof of posting, for instance, or insure the goods in transit at their own cost.' Some sellers in the clothing or footwear business, where returns are expected, supply pre-printed return labels. You don't have to go to those lengths, but make sure returns are organized and easy to deal with at both ends.

Many big online retailers refund without question within a certain period, and as a result some buyers have grown used to thinking that they can send a purchase back not only if they find something wrong with it, but also if they simply change their mind. The one site where people understand that this principle doesn't apply is eBay, where the rules make it clear that once you have bid successfully, you cannot return the item unless it is faulty or not as described. Even on eBay, however, buyers sometimes try to get a refund for no other reason than that they don't like the item now that it is in their possession.

Don't put off dealing with the issue. Most disputes escalate because someone has put the problem to one side and not replied to the buyer's complaint. It's a mistake to imagine that if someone has complained, you've automatically lost their future business, so why make the effort of appeasing them? Sort it right away, and you can often leave the customer feeling even happier with you and coming back for more, because your response was prompt and *you said sorry*. It's a tiny word, but an apology really matters, and doesn't cost you anything.

So the trick to testing a sales system is to visualize the customer journey every step of the way, from search through payment and delivery to complaint handling.

'Everyone makes mistakes occasionally,' says Tom Norris. 'Even the big boys – in fact they make them even more often! Through no fault of your own, you'll send stuff out that doesn't work. A plant that dies in transit, maybe, or something that is damaged in the post. Maybe Royal Mail loses the package or they stick it in the wrong letter box. Your customer won't see that as the carrier's problem – they'll blame *you* for failing to deliver. Online sellers have to own the whole process, and be ready to solve problems quickly and cheerfully, so the customer will be happy to come back to buy more in the future.'

TOP TIPS

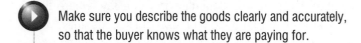 Make sure you describe the goods clearly and accurately, so that the buyer knows what they are paying for.

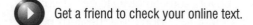 Get a friend to check your online text.

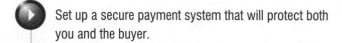 Set up a secure payment system that will protect both you and the buyer.

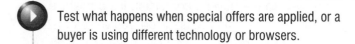 Test what happens when special offers are applied, or a buyer is using different technology or browsers.

Organize your dispatch system, and keep your delivery promises.

Make paperwork handling simple and efficient.

Check the carrier is handling deliveries competently.

Think through your returns policy and make sure the customer understands it.

Don't procrastinate or ignore complaints!

Own the whole process, and always be prepared to apologize, even if it isn't your fault.

QUESTION

What do I do if my business is more successful than
I expected, and I'm swamped with orders?

Wouldn't we all love a problem like that! But dream sales
can turn into a nightmare if you don't act rapidly.

Don't leave customers dangling without knowing what's
happening to their order. Send out e-mails to everyone
who has ordered. Often they will be very reasonable if
you explain to them there's been unprecedented demand,
and that their goods will arrive eventually. You could offer
them an instant refund if they don't want to wait – most
will happily hang on. In the meantime, take on more staff
if you can afford it, to get those orders moving as
quickly as possible.

ACTIVITY

Persuade one of your friends to act as a 'secret shopper'
and order something from your website. You can always
give them the money to do so provided they give the
item back!

You want to be absolutely sure that everything is going
to work in an organized, efficient way and it is only by
testing your systems that you can be certain that the
shopping experience for your customers is going to
work well.

PART II
SELLING THINGS LARGE AND SMALL

CHAPTER 4
SELLING VIA AMAZON

Amazon is one of the best-known global online retailers. Millions of people visit its site every day. It now sells products in over 20 different categories, from baby clothes to CDs and DVDs, but it began with the simple and brilliant idea of making itself into the biggest bookshop in the world. For many people that's exactly what Amazon is – first choice for book buying.

SELLING BOOKS ON AMAZON

Lots of us dream of becoming a best-selling author. Landing a publishing deal isn't easy – congratulations if you have one! But whether or not you have a publisher lined up, or if you plan to self-publish a book, you can still add to your sales by making sure your book has an online presence. Of course, you could simply promote it and sell it through your own website – but book buyers usually start their search for a book through one of the big online retailers. Besides, if you sell through Amazon you don't have to worry about setting up your own payment system or protecting yourself against online payment fraud – Amazon looks after all of that for you.

And even if you love books but don't have a creative bone in your body or any desire to write one, you could still make money on Amazon by trading in second-hand books: collecting and selling signed first editions, perhaps, or even just reselling books you bought from the site and want to clear from your shelves.

In this chapter you will learn:

- how to go about getting your book on Amazon;
- what other products you can sell through the site;
- the different choices you have as a seller;
- how even established authors whose publishers handle their marketing and sales can make money from Amazon;
- how to earn yourself 10 per cent of the selling price of any product on Amazon.

CASE STUDY

Olympic women

Stephanie Daniels and Anita Tedder are passionate about sport. They met when they were training as PE teachers in Bedford. Later, Steph decided to take her studies further and do a master's degree. She made a special study of women who had taken part in the early days of the modern Olympic Games, when many sports excluded women. In the first modern Olympics, for instance, in 1896, no women at all took any official part in the contests. (There was one unofficial female competitor, but you'll have to buy the book to find out how she sneaked in!)

Steph and Anita travelled all over the world to find women who had taken part in the Olympics before the Second World War. The stories they uncovered were so fascinating that they decided to write a book based on Steph's research. There were women who had swum for England in the 1920s or fenced for the United States; women who had been offered Hollywood film work based on their sporting prowess; women who had been there at the notorious Olympic Games in Berlin in 1936 presided over by Hitler, when the stadium was filled with swastikas, and the black athlete Jesse Owens created an enormous stir by winning a gold medal and overturning Nazi theories of racial supremacy.

Steph and Anita self-published their book, *A Proper Spectacle: Women Olympians 1900–36*. It was expensive to produce, as it contained a lot of pictures, but they have nearly recouped all their costs by selling it online.

'We sold them initially through our website, www.olympic-women.co.uk,' says Anita. 'What was great was to send them worldwide and to make contact with other historians, who were the main buyers. We only went with Amazon after we had some problems with our payment system and became busy with other work.'

Now they generate sales through both routes. They continue to sell the book through their own website, using PayPal. Those sales they still pack and deliver themselves, signing the book if the buyer requests it, but with Amazon they use a system called Fulfilment, so delivery is handled for them.

'Our aim was only ever to cover our costs and to tell a story we thought should be told. It has led to vast riches, but none of them financial! The wonderful thing is all the people we have met or exchanged e-mails with, as a result of the book.'

Anita and Steph have made money online from an enthusiasm that has attracted other enthusiasts for the same subject. Few books make big money, and a lot don't so much as break even. But Anita and Steph's example shows how you can make a self-published book pay for itself – and make friends all over the world along the way!

For people who write a book about their area of professional expertise, there are spin-off rewards too, as Simon Standish's story shows.

CASE STUDY

Simon Standish

Simon Standish is a management consultant who specializes in leadership development, project management and showing companies how to deal with change. He runs his own business called Change FX, and his clients include private, public and voluntary sector organizations, many in the field of health and well-being services. With an MBA and 30 years' experience behind him, and having worked for well-known firms such as PricewaterhouseCoopers and Kingsley Lord, Simon decided to write a book called *People, Projects and Change*, a practical book about project management.

'It's a good calling card,' he says. 'For me it was satisfying to be able to condense all the things I've learned into a book, and pass them on, but writing a book about your area of expertise gives you credibility. People think: he's written a book about it, so he must know what he's talking about.'

Many of the copies he's sold have been bought directly from him by clients. But not long ago he decided he would also sell the book online through Amazon.

'The main reason was because it gives you a presence. When people go on the internet and type in my name on Google, the Amazon reference will be high on the list that comes up. They'll know immediately that I have a book for sale, and won't have to wade through a load of other references first.'

But that wasn't the only thing he felt Amazon had to offer. 'What I admire is their sophistication in the way they communicate to customers. They collect customers' preferences, and use that to alert them to other books that might interest them. If a customer has bought a business book before, when they next go on Amazon they'll find recommendations taking them to similar books – which might include mine. And when you look up a specific book on the site, they tell you what other people looking at the same book have bought. I've even had e-mails from them saying "You bought that, would you also be interested in this?" It's a clever system that markets the book for you, and doesn't only promote bestsellers.'

When Simon decided to use Amazon to sell his book, it took him less than a couple of hours to make the arrangements. 'All you do is visit the sales side of their website, and click the *Sell on Amazon* button. A number of e-mails went to and fro, but it wasn't burdensome at all. And once you've gone through the initial set-up and registered one book, you can just keep adding titles!'

Simon also registered for an Amazon feature called *Search inside*. This lets customers look inside the book via the website – a bit like pulling a book off the shelf in a bookshop and flicking through the pages to see if it's what you want. People can't browse the whole book, but they can examine the contents page and look at a sample chapter. It's another way of helping persuade a prospective customer your book is exactly what they're after.

Simon found there were a number of different choices about how to sell through Amazon. There were different rates, based on the number and type of items you expect to sell, but basically, under the arrangement he made, he gets 40 per cent of the listed purchase price, less postage and packing costs. He could choose whether to handle the deliveries of the books himself, or let Amazon deliver for him through Fulfilment.

'That turned out to be more of a hassle than I had expected. I don't regret doing it, but you have to realize that it does involve a certain amount of administration. The way Amazon keep their costs down is by not storing huge numbers of books. For small fry like me, they only want to hold a couple of copies at a time in their storage facility, rather than hundreds. So every so often, I get an e-mail asking me to send them more books – but it'll never be a complete box of books they want, unfortunately. They might ask for five or six, or they might ask only for one or two. The end result is that it takes a fair bit of my time managing the flow of books, because as soon as they send an e-mail asking for more, you have to verify you've received the order, and dispatch the books almost immediately: they usually stipulate a 48-hour turnaround. If I go away on holiday, I have to set up contingencies so someone else will pick up the e-mails and respond on my behalf. So although in theory having them handle delivery saves you running backwards and forwards to the post office all the time, it doesn't do away with the administration, and that can be a burden if you're only a small company or a one-man band, doing this on the side.'

But in spite of this, he's delighted with the way selling on Amazon has worked out for him. 'I went into this with open eyes, and I never expected to make my fortune from selling my book. But putting it on Amazon has generated a good few orders, and raised its profile. I've even had enquiries from as far afield as Japan – Amazon don't only put the book on their UK site; it's ended up on the US and German sites, as well as Amazon Japan. I didn't ask for that – it just happened! So I've been able to sell my book, and my services, all over the world.'

So how do you go about selling via an online retailer like Amazon? It's very, very simple, as Simon says, and only takes a short time to set up. (What takes the time is writing a book in the first place!)

But many people who write books self-publish; they pay someone to design and print the book, while handling the sales side themselves. If that's you, Amazon is a great site to sell from because it is so well known, and has become virtually a generic name for book sales online. It gives your book real credibility, and you'll feel proud as Punch seeing it up there on the site along with all the other millions of books Amazon sells.

WHAT ELSE CAN YOU SELL ON AMAZON?

You can sell brand new books via Amazon, or second-hand ones. The company has expanded into many other products and you can use the site for selling anything from exercise balls to kitchen equipment. Take a look at the categories you are allowed to sell in:

- Books;
- Music;
- DVDs;
- VHS;
- Baby;
- Electronics and Computing;
- Home and Garden;
- Shoes;
- Software;

- Sports and Leisure;
- DIY and Tools;
- PC and Video Games.

Toys and games are also allowed but there are restrictions on selling these around Christmas time.

Provided you get prior approval from Amazon, you could also sell clothing, health and beauty items, and jewellery and watches.

HOW TO START THE PROCESS

The first step is to go to the website: Amazon.co.uk. Don't be put off by the fact that the home page looks as if it is purely for shoppers. Scroll down to the bottom, and you will see a heading, *Make Money with Us*, and under that a link to *Sell on Amazon*.

Have to hand the details of:

- your credit card;
- your telephone number;
- bank account information;
- in the European Union, a VAT number if your company is VAT registered, or elsewhere corresponding details for whatever sales tax applies;
- An e-mail address.

You will also need to provide product information – title description and so on – plus an image of the product, its price, and the EAN, UPC, or ISBN code – the unique number allotted to every book when it is published.

HOW TO FIND YOUR WAY THROUGH THE DIFFERENT CHOICES YOU HAVE AS A SELLER

Keep in mind what you want to achieve and you will have no difficulty sorting out the right choice for you.

The first decision you need to make is whether to register yourself as a casual seller or a professional seller. Casual, or individual, sellers are those who are likely to shift less than 35 items a month, and if you choose this option you will be charged a small fee per sale, plus a referral or closing fee of 17.25 per cent of the purchase price. If you are selling second-hand books this might well be the best option to start with, as you pay nothing up front, but only start handing money to Amazon when you have sold an item. You can always upgrade later if you find that you're selling more than 35 items a month.

The snag with this option is that you can only use it to sell items that are already in the Amazon catalogue, such as second-hand books or used items. That won't apply to a book you've written and self-published. So in that case you'll have to go for the other choice: professional seller, or pro-merchant.

Professional sellers are those who expect to sell more than 35 items a month, and instead they are charged a flat-rate monthly subscription fee, no matter how many items they sell. There's no long-term commitment and you can cancel any time you want to. On top of that, you will pay a variable fee per item sold, depending on the type of product sold and where it is being dispatched to. This is where the numbers get complicated, but if you're selling a book, the fee is calculated in two parts: a referral fee, which will be 17.25 per cent of the product price (15 per cent if you are based within a European Union country and have received a VAT registration number from the country where your business is registered), plus a variable closing fee, which depends on where the book is going to.

The Amazon website will direct you to simple tables that explain the different fees based on what kind of product you are selling.

THE NEXT STEPS

Once you have registered with Amazon and given them your details, it's easy to upload your inventory via the web-based interface, a free desktop software application. As soon as an order is placed via the Amazon website, you receive an e-mail notifying you of the customer's details, and you then pack and deliver the item to the customer. You are covered by Amazon's fraud protection, so there is no need to worry. Payment for the order is deposited by Amazon into your bank account, and you will receive a notification by e-mail that payment has been sent. Usually your seller's account is settled every 14 days, and it will then take five business days until the money arrives in your bank account.

If your customer is unhappy with the product, they will contact you in the first instance, but in the event of a dispute, Amazon will step in to resolve the issue. Remember, just like eBay, it's vital that you keep your side of the bargain as a seller, because there is a system of customer feedback on Amazon. Maintaining a high feedback rating is essential, or people won't want to buy from you!

SORTING OUT A DELIVERY SYSTEM

Under the basic deal for both of these options – individual seller or pro-merchant – you handle the deliveries yourself. That's probably the best option if you are selling second-hand books, for instance.

Anita and Steph chose an additional option for the books they sold through Amazon: the Fulfilment service. This is the way to go if you don't want to be bothered with trotting down to the post office or arranging a courier every time you receive an order. Instead, Amazon handles all the deliveries for you, packing and shipping the product direct to the customer. It's only available if you register as a pro-merchant, though.

An advantage is that people trust Amazon to deliver, so this option might win you extra sales. The downside, as Simon pointed out, is that although Amazon will hold stocks of your book in the warehouse, in order to keep their costs down they don't keep more than a few copies at a time. If they decide to restock, you are obliged to send them more copies right away! So you could find yourself making almost as many trips to the post office as someone who has decided to handle deliveries themselves.

FURTHER CHOICES

But there's a further option you could upgrade to for book sales if you are a self-published author expecting to shift reasonable numbers of books, or if you are a publisher, studio or recording label, a distributor for other people's creative product, be it a book, music or video. This option is called Amazon Advantage, and it's a similar kind of deal to the one the big publishers negotiate. Simon signed up for this, because it does carry some real pluses that may make your book more attractive to buyers. The terms are different and don't at first look as advantageous financially, though if you make a realistic assessment of what sales you can expect you might well end up making more this way. You agree the list price with Amazon, who guarantee you 40 per cent of that figure, minus packing and delivery costs.

The first big plus is that books sold via Advantage show as in stock and available immediately, rather than in six weeks' time, which is the standard description under other arrangements.

Amazon can then decide to discount it, which will make it more attractive still to buyers.

You also get quick payment terms, and you can list items that are not yet published or released, in order to create advance interest in your creative product.

If you choose to sell via Amazon Advantage, take some time to think carefully about the price of your book, CD or DVD. Check out what other people are selling similar items for. Be realistic! There are people who will pay a higher price for a book on a specialist subject, but if you are hoping to sell a self-published novel, you can't hope to shift many copies if it costs more than other fiction.

HOW TO MAKE MONEY ON AMAZON BY DOING ALMOST NOTHING AT ALL

The final option is for people who want to sell on Amazon via their own website. You can choose to become an Associate. Basically, this means that you set up a link to Amazon from your site. You will receive up to 10 per cent of the selling price every time someone clicks and buys via that link. Effectively, you are advertising Amazon products for them, and they will provide you with tools to create customized text, or text and image links, or you can use Amazon banners.

This is a really useful option for authors whose publishers are handling the marketing of their book for them, but who would still like to make a little extra money on the side. When you set up your own website, make sure your fans can buy your books through it by creating a link to your book on Amazon. You can even give your fans the choice of which online retailer they buy from, by creating similar affiliate links to other online bookstores such as W H Smith or Waterstones.

It's also a good way of making money out of your website whatever the content. Suppose you run an enthusiasts' website that specializes in the history of tank warfare, and one of your members has written a book about British tanks of the Second World War. You could help him sell books by including a link to his book on Amazon, and your site will get paid every time a sale is made. Or perhaps you are a young mum who runs a site for other young mums. Why not build in a link to Amazon's Toys, Kids or Baby departments? Or to a baby book on their site that really helped you?

The possibilities are endless. Be creative – you don't have to write a book to sell on Amazon!

Step-by-step guide:

- What are you going to sell? Check it fits in Amazon's categories.
- With your bank details and other information, go to Amazon.co.uk (or your local Amazon website if you

live outside the UK) and click on *Sell on Amazon* at the bottom of the page.

- Decide how many items you will be selling a month.
- If fewer than 35, opt for casual seller (second-hand books and other items already in the Amazon catalogue).
- If more than 35, consider registering as a professional seller.
- Do you want to handle deliveries yourself, or have Amazon do this for you – in which case, select their Fulfilment service.
- For authors, publishers, studios and distributors of creative product (books, CDs, DVDs, etc) consider Amazon Advantage: you will get 40 per cent of the list price you set and quicker payment.
- Become an Associate and make money by including a link to Amazon on your own website.

TOP TIPS

 Amazon has become the generic name for book sales online.

 Even if you have self-published, it gives your book real credibility.

 All you do is visit the sales side of their website, and click the *Sell on Amazon* button.

 A number of e-mails help you get registered.

Once you've gone through the initial set-up and registered one book, you can just keep adding titles.

 It's easier to sell the book (and quicker) than to write it.

QUESTION

 How do I get my payment via Amazon?

As soon as an order is placed via the Amazon website, you receive an e-mail notifying you of the customer's details, and you then pack and deliver the item to the customer. Payment for the order is deposited by Amazon into your bank account, and you will receive a notification by e-mail that payment has been sent. Usually your seller's account is settled every 14 days, and it will then take five business days until the money arrives in your bank account.

ACTIVITY

 Register yourself on Amazon as a casual, or individual, seller – you have nothing to loose, as you pay nothing up front, but only start handing money to Amazon when you have sold an item. You can always upgrade to professional seller later if you find that you're selling more than 35 items a month.

CHAPTER 5
SELLING A HOUSE ONLINE

What if you want to sell something really big online – a house?

Lots of people dream of beating the system and resent having to pay fees for an estate agent or realtor to sell their home for them. After all, what does an estate agent actually do to earn their percentage? Take a few pictures, upload them to their website, then show people round? How hard is that?

A professional would rightly point out that it is a lot harder than you think, that their job is backed up by years of experience in marketing and selling houses, and that they take away the hassle and save you from making mistakes. Fair enough. But if you're still game to give it a try, you can save a shedload of money by cutting out High Street agents and marketing your house wholly online. Often buyers don't much like estate agents either, and would prefer to bypass them. They think they get in the way, and artificially push prices up. Indeed, many buyers expect to get better value by dealing with a private seller.

In this chapter you will learn:

- the difference between private sale websites and online estate agents;
- what kind of sites will help your house be seen by the greatest possible number of potential buyers;
- how to decide the right price;
- how to prepare photos and marketing material that make your house look great;
- and how to best present your property when you show people round.

CASE STUDY

Rhonda Bewsey

A few years ago, Rhonda and her husband decided to move from the UK to Spain. 'It was the life we'd always dreamed of,' says Rhonda. 'Sun all year round, easy access to the sea or mountains. We loved the place and the people, and we'd found the perfect home.'

Having bought in Spain, all they had to do to complete the move was to sell their property in the UK. The market at the time was booming, but Rhonda resented having to pay a percentage of the sale price to an agent. So the couple decided to try and sell their home online, through a private house sale site.

'We spotted an ad for it in a national newspaper, and it seemed like a brilliant idea,' says Rhonda. 'The one we used was HouseWeb, who charge a flat fee. No estate agents' percentages – we calculated we would save literally thousands of pounds.'

HouseWeb was the first UK-based private house sale site, established in 1996, and advertising property both in the UK and abroad. Now they have a number of competitors. Most work on a similar basis, offering different levels of service depending on the fee you pay. HouseWeb offered Rhonda and her husband three options: a standard service at a very low fee, a deluxe service for rather more, and at top whack, a platinum package. They went for the middle, deluxe, option.

'The standard service was cheap but basic,' says Rhonda. 'It advertised your property on their site, with one photo and a link to a Google location map, and the ad stays until the house is sold. But we felt the key to attracting buyers was to display a number of photos, showing the property at its best. The deluxe package allowed six photos. The other advantage of upgrading was that not only did your ad appear on HouseWeb's site, it also appeared on several other national property sites, including Fish4Homes, and you could have a link in the ad to your own website, so you could create a more detailed online brochure for yourself, which is what we did. The platinum service gave you a few more benefits, like 25 photos, a personalized "For Sale" board to put up, and you could be listed as their Feature Property of the Week on their main page, but we felt the deluxe was enough for us.'

Like many other private house sale sites, this one offered the protection of a secure messaging service, so that although prospective buyers contact you via e-mail, your own e-mail address is not revealed, protecting you against spam and malicious mail.

Rhonda and her husband made sure they put the right price on the property by inviting two estate agents to value it, then picking a figure between the two valuations.

'Of course, we ourselves had to do most of the jobs a selling agent does,' says Rhonda. 'We had to take our own photos, write our own description of the property, and show people round ourselves. But I liked that. It meant we had control, and it was the idea of being in total control as well as saving a packet that was the deciding factor. I've always believed the knack to selling is to have really lovely photos and good written content, and I reckoned we could do at least as good a job as an agent and probably a lot better. We took loads of pictures on our digital camera and chose the very best to put on the website, and I wrote a description that made the property sound attractive, but without so much detail the reader became bored.'

It worked. The property sold within a couple of weeks. Rhonda and her husband were thrilled. 'It saved us thousands, and we managed to save even more money by using an online conveyancing service too. I wouldn't have done that if we had been buying at the same time, but since we were only selling it was a fairly simple transaction, and you could see immediately online where you were in the process and what documents had been received.'

Would she do the same again? 'I guess it would depend on the state of the housing market at the time. It worked well for us because the market was strong and there was a huge demand for houses. But the principle is a good one, and if you can find a site that will attract plenty of potential buyers, who wouldn't want to save that much money?'

So what do the professionals say about selling online? No estate agent or realtor is going to be in favour of buyers going it alone, but some independent property experts argue that it is as good a way of selling as any, if you are prepared to put the work in.

Gavin Brazg runs an impartial advisory service for people who want to sell their house online. He knows the housing market well, having trained as an architect and then worked for a well-known UK house-building company, putting together residential developments.

'The fact is that you aren't really selling a house online,' he says. 'The house only sells when someone walks through the front door and decides this is the right property for them. What you are doing is *marketing* it online – and that's exactly what estate agents do! It's simply the most effective way of getting a property ad in front of the largest number of buyers possible – 90 per cent of buyers start their search via an online property portal. All the rest – the ads in the High Street window, the "For Sale" board, the glossy brochure – is done solely for the benefit of the estate agent or realtor. These are not really tools to attract buyers, it's the agent's way of establishing awareness of their brand – and why should you pay for that?'

GETTING STARTED

You will need to market your property through a specialist website. It isn't enough to build your own website and hope potential buyers stumble across it when they Google 'homes for sale' in a particular area. The only buyers you will attract that way are companies looking to buy properties quickly for cash, at rock-bottom prices below market value.

Gavin's advice, in a less active housing market than the one Rhonda sold in, is to look for an online property site that will not only advertise your home for you on its own site, but also act as a gateway to the big property sites the estate agents use to sell houses.

'In the UK, for instance, one of the main property sites is RightMove,' he says. 'That and maybe a couple of others are the first places most buyers look. Some even sign up for alerts from the site when a property matching their needs comes on the market. So you want to make sure your property is there too, not stuck on some out-of-the-way private website that few people visit.'

The big property websites like RightMove in the UK don't allow private individuals to advertise with them. Your ad will only appear there if you find an online estate agent that has an arrangement with them. Online estate agents are not the same as High Street agents who happen to have an online presence. A true online agent will, like the private house sale sites, only charge you a flat fee, whatever the price of your property. The fee will be higher than the private house sale sites charge, but still only a tenth or less of what you would pay in commission to an agent demanding a percentage.

Again, you will be in control of taking the photos of your property and writing the text, though some of the bigger online agents will do that for you too – at a price! They have local reps who will come and value your property for you, and even arrange viewings and show potential buyers round, but usually that will be your job.

Law and custom on buying and selling vary hugely depending on where in the world the property is, and there isn't room for us to include an exhaustive country-by-country guide. But make sure you understand the laws that govern property transactions in the country where your property is located – especially if you are selling property abroad, where you may not be so familiar with the ins and outs of property law.

'Wherever in the world you live, there are just two things that sell a property,' says Gavin Brazg. 'Pricing it correctly, and presenting it well.'

HOW DO YOU KNOW WHAT PRICE TO ASK?

Here you do need professional advice from people who know the market in your area. Fortunately this is usually the one service you can get for free from a local agent or realtor! Unless you plan to place your ad with one of the bigger online estate agents who also offer a valuation service, all you need do is ring up at least three of the leading High Street agents in your area. Ask them to come and value your property because you are thinking of putting it on the market. Schedule them all one after another for the same day, so they see the property under the same conditions.

There is often a surprising measure of agreement in the figures they come up with, but don't give in to temptation and go for the highest price suggested! Remember, they want your business, so they may be telling you what they think you want to hear, rather than putting a realistic price on the property. When you think you have found that realistic figure by comparing valuations, consider whether to drop a little below it when you advertise online. After all you're saving money by not using one of these agents, so you can afford to advertise at a lower price to attract more viewings. Remember, many buyers expect to get better value by dealing with a private seller.

But don't value it too low, or people may conclude you're desperate to sell, or that there's something wrong with the property!

While they're there, ask the High Street agents what they think are the strong and weak points of the property, and whether it is worth doing anything about them. Those tired old kitchen units – should they be replaced? It's probably not worth it, though the price will have to reflect the state of them. You can pick up useful hints and tips about what will help sell your property, from taking down net curtains to planting pots of summer bedding round the front door.

Those agents who value your property are going to be very persuasive. They will tell you what a hassle it is trying to sell without an agent, and they may use the argument that their percentages are on a no-sale-no-fee basis. What, you might think, have I got to lose? – especially if there is some urgency about the sale. Why not go for both and let the agent advertise it at the same time as you advertise it yourself through one of the cheaper private websites?

Beware! You must read the small print of the agent's contract, because many insist on sole-agency rights – and that means that even if you succeed in selling it privately without their help they can still demand you pay them. The onus will be on you to show that the buyer was attracted to the property *only* through the ad on the private website, and that may be hard to prove. There have been cases in the UK where people took their house off a local estate agent's books and off the market entirely, then sold a few months later privately to friends, only to find that the agent chased them through the courts for a cut.

PHOTOGRAPHING AND PRESENTING YOUR HOUSE

Once you have decided on the price, tackle the presentation. That means getting some really good photos of the property to put on the web ad. Don't settle for a few hasty snaps on your mobile phone. Borrow a good camera, and wait for a sunny day before you photograph the exterior of the property and the garden, if you have one. Choose a good angle, so that eyesores like the neighbour's sagging fence or the electricity substation next door don't appear in the shot. People will of course see them when they come to view the property, but you don't want to put them off before they get there.

A useful trick is to augment the ad on the online agent's website with a link to your own personal website as a kind of 'online brochure' for the property. You can use it to go into much more detail, both in the photos and the descriptions. Don't forget to tell people if you are in the catchment area for a particularly popular school, and about the amenities in the area, like nearby swimming pools or shops. You can even make a video walk-through of your property and upload it to your website. For more information on how to do this, see *A Quick Start Guide to Podcasting*, published by Kogan Page.

Indoors, turn on table lamps when you take photos to give each room a warm glow even in daylight, and remove as much clutter as possible, rearranging the furniture if necessary or even moving some of it out to display the room at its best. A fish-eye lens helps make a small room look bigger.

If your home has period features, photograph these in close-up. The detail from a carved newel post or colourful art nouveau fireplace tiles are worth showing off, and make a contrast with the wider room views.

For as long as it takes to sell it, you will have to make your home as much like a show home as you can. It will be worth it the long run. Be ready to whisk your son's dirty football kit into a cupboard at a moment's notice. Don't leave wet washing hanging about the place. Keep the place tidy and uncluttered, the lawn mown, and leave out only the kind of personal possessions that will appeal to the buyers you hope to attract. A Harley in the garage is great, but a Kawasaki in bits on the front lawn is a definite no!

What you are selling in these photos is a lifestyle choice as much as a home. Most people are aiming to move up the property ladder. They want a property they can picture themselves in, enjoying the lifestyle they aspire to. A friend of mine admits she was attracted to the cottage she eventually bought because the photographer had cleverly included next door's soft-top Morris Minor in the picture.

Good luck!

TOP TIPS

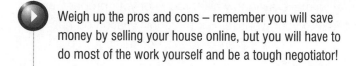 Weigh up the pros and cons – remember you will save money by selling your house online, but you will have to do most of the work yourself and be a tough negotiator!

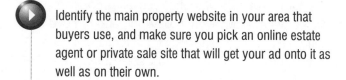 Identify the main property website in your area that buyers use, and make sure you pick an online estate agent or private sale site that will get your ad onto it as well as on their own.

 Set your price by getting several valuations from local agents.

Don't just go for the highest figure – buyers expect a price reduction if you cut out the middleman.

Take the best photos you can to show your property at its best.

Set-dress viewings by putting out fresh flowers – you're selling a lifestyle as much as a home.

De-clutter and keep your house clean and bright.

Remember, it's only for a few weeks until those offers roll in!

Be streetwise when arranging viewings.

Stay calm in negotiation.

Be willing to compromise.

QUESTION

Are estate agents ripping off home sellers?

No! Although you might resent having to pay fees for an estate agent or realtor to sell your home, it is a lot harder than you think. Their job is backed up by years of experience in marketing and selling houses, and they take away the hassle and save you from making mistakes.

ACTIVITY

Look for an online property site that will not only advertise your home for you on its own site, but also act as a gateway to the big property sites the estate agents use to sell houses.

Different countries have different property sites. You need to find the best so that your property is there too, not stuck on some out-of-the-way website that few people visit.

PART III
SELLING INTANGIBLES: IDEAS AND CREATIVITY

CHAPTER 6
MAKING MONEY FROM INFORMATION

Everything you've learned so far in this book has been about making money from selling physical objects, like farm produce or an unwanted electric guitar, or creative products like a book or music.

But can you also make money out of intangibles? Out of ideas, or information, stuff you can't physically wrap up and deliver?

The answer, of course, is yes, and lots of people are doing it already. You'll probably have been to their websites. You may not even have realized that they are making money – but take it from me, there is very little that comes entirely free, not even on the internet, whatever people would like you to believe!

The internet began with the great notion that information should be free. But if something is available without you paying for it up front, it doesn't necessarily mean that it comes at no cost, or that people aren't making money from it somehow! Some of the web's earliest pioneers were laid-back Californian geeks who believed passionately that people should be able to swap ideas and information freely. Those guys still dress like hippies, eat beansprouts and drink wheat juice, but they're millionaires now. Some of them are billionaires.

The great debate at the moment is how to monetize content. A generation has grown up believing that they are entitled to free software, free music, free news, free advice. That's a terrific idea, but it doesn't take into account that it costs money and time to develop and provide these things. Somehow it all has to be paid for, and even idealists are happier if they can make a profit as well. They know that if you don't want to be rich, you can plough the money back into developing something else.

Some big players, like Rupert Murdoch with his global company News Corporation, have decided that the way to go is to charge the customer directly for content. Others, like Alan Rusbridger, editor of the UK's *Guardian* newspaper, have decided that the information itself should be free, but that money can be generated in other ways to pay for it.

The one commodity the internet thrives on more than any other is information. You might be passionate about a particular sport, for instance, and set up a site to provide news and a discussion forum for like-minded fans. Or perhaps you have a collection of crop-circle photographs that would attract other enthusiasts all over the world, or you might want to share information on a particular medical condition. Even if you only want to raise enough to break even on the costs of setting up and maintaining the website, there are ways of generating revenue streams from the most esoteric information. If you have an interest or a passion, why not make money out of it?

In this chapter you will learn:

- how you can generate income while offering something that the customer doesn't directly pay for;

- how to provide content tailored to a target group of consumers;
- how to build a team to help you;
- how to form partnerships with like-minded companies to monetize an intangible.

CASE STUDY

Emiel Van Melis and Sideways News

Emiel Van Melis is a man with a passion. He loves news. But he's not just your average information junkie – Emiel believes that news shouldn't just be consumed passively, it should make you want to get out of your chair and do something about the state of the world!

When Emiel looked at the news that was available online, he could see that there was a gap in the market. For breaking news, people would go to sites like that run by the BBC – British in origin, but a global brand that is trusted all over the world. He couldn't hope to compete with an outfit like that, which has teams of journalists on every continent providing an up-to-the minute service. Then there were plenty of specialist news operations, again run by established news 'brands' like the *Economist* or *New Scientist*. These were publications that long ago established their reputation in print before opening online outlets, and knew their patch inside out.

'I didn't want to duplicate what those publications were doing, and doing very well,' he says. 'I thought we could be something in the middle – topical, but not running to keep up in providing breaking news, informed but not necessarily intensely deep and specialist. The basic idea was that a lot of people have a need for a different kind of news: a broader range of subjects than you normally get in mainstream news. They want an active, positive angle on what's happening – they're fed up with sensationalist, negative news, celebrity hype, gossip.'

A start-up online news operation might sound ambitious, but there are precedents for what Emiel hoped to do. There are other sites that began on the internet as outlets for specialist blogs, and have gone on to establish a successful news brand: in the United States, the Huffington Post and Politico, for example.

Emiel is from Holland, but he was thinking beyond the borders of his native land. He wanted to build a news brand that was truly international. So he decided the site should be in the English language rather than Dutch, and began his market research in the UK.

'We identified gradually that our target group was really the so-called "cultural creatives", of whom there are an estimated 50 million in the United States now and 80 million in Europe,' he says. 'We pulled a lot of market research from the internet, and also did our own using focus groups. The clear message was that these people wanted news that was not negative or sensationalist: they wanted to read coverage that was geared towards solutions rather than underlining problems all the time.'

To highlight how the website offers a different take on the world, Emiel and his team have called it Sideways News. Another key difference is that every story is written so that it carries what Emiel describes as 'a call to action'.

'We have a pillar on the site header entitled *Taking Action*, which encourages our visitors to champion a cause, donate money or give time to volunteering, across a broad spectrum of issues. It doesn't just have a green focus, it covers the whole gamut of questions cultural creatives care about, and contains links to other sites we think are of interest. The fact that we are action-orientated is our key USP – unique selling point – compared with other news providers.'

The site already has visitors from 180 countries worldwide, of which the 'top five' are the UK, the United States, Canada,

India and the Netherlands. 'Our target group is the well-educated, enquiring optimist, interested in issues like social justice, population growth and sustainability. These are people who also happen to be quite affluent.'

That was the key foundation of the business model. He could attract a committed 'niche' audience interested in the kind of issues explored on the website, demonstrably willing to come back again and again. These affluent consumers represented a high-premium group of interest to companies offering products geared to similar people. Emiel did not need to sell information to his customers – instead he could sell space on his site to other organizations, so that they could sell things to his target audience.

Building an information brand doesn't happen overnight. Emiel took time to perfect the website to attract the right kind of consumers, though it is now up and running and already generating income. 'Sideways News took a lot of investment up front to build a good product,' he says. 'The value will come from the brand in future years. But we're on our way: we have a proper business with a number of investors on board because they are impressed with what we have done already. It's expanding all the time.'

So how can you follow Emiel's example and make money out of information? Sideways News has found its own market of ethically minded cultural creatives, but there is nothing to stop you coming up with your own idea and setting up a site that will appeal to another niche group of information seekers. If the content is compelling, and you can attract a core audience in sufficient numbers to entice advertisers, you can even monetize your blog.

MEASURE AND TEST

Your first step, having decided what kind of information you want to provide on the site, is to identify your target group and what kind of service they will want from the site. If you are planning to set up a business to generate a strong revenue stream from the site, investing in some serious market research is a good idea.

Emiel used a market research agency to set up a series of focus groups, who were shown mock-ups of the website and asked to react to possible brand names. That helped hone the way Sideways News would present content to its target group.

But you can start small and carry out your own market research by contacting people you know who share your interest. Ask them what they would like to find on the site. Indeed, you can continue to research and perfect the content after you are up and running, by asking visitors to send you feedback or fill in questionnaires.

Emiel's team continued to refine Sideways News after they had built the website by sitting people down at a PC with a webcam focused on their eyes, to discover what part of the page they looked at first and how they moved around the site.

'Online, everything is measurable,' says Emiel. 'Test every step, measure things and if you see it works, take it to the next level.'

Through tools like Google Analytics, you can see where visitors to your site come from, how long they spend on it, which pages they look at, and other useful information that will help you understand your audience and their needs, and perfect the way your site works.

BUILD A TEAM

Your site may be small enough to run on your own, but every online enterprise benefits from having the right team behind it. Look for people whose talent and expertise will complement your own, rather than duplicate it.

Emiel's strengths were in marketing and sales, and he had entrepreneurial experience as well from previous ventures, as did his business partner. What they both lacked was in-depth online experience, so he recruited the former online publishing head of Virgin Media, who was also able to provide guidance on writing skills and journalism. But the site is also about community action, so they brought in a team member with strengths in community management. Finally they enlisted the talents of a journalist who also had e-commerce and sales experience.

'If you don't have the right people on your team or the right partners, it can really slow you down,' says Emiel. And as he later discovered, it's essential to be prepared to get rid of anyone who isn't pulling their weight. 'After a number of months we decided we had to walk away from the original web builder, because the relationship just wasn't working out – he wasn't reliable. But then maybe another member of the team will recommend somebody they've worked with before, whom you would never have come across otherwise. The lesson for me was that it's really important with every person to check them out thoroughly and make sure that they will be able to provide the skills you need, or it could waste a lot of your start-up money and set you back months.'

REVENUE SOURCES

The simplest way of making money from information is to set up a subscription site, so that people either pay to access it or are charged every time they download an article. But although this model can work well for established sites like libraries and specialist publications, it is of little use for a new information provider starting out small.

Sideways News rejected the idea of subscriptions. 'We have four revenue streams,' says Emiel. 'The first and most obvious is advertising – selling space on the site for other companies to advertise their wares to your target group.'

If you are going to sell space on your site to advertisers, it is a good idea to find ones whose products will be a good fit with the kind of content you offer. So a holiday information website might look for advertisers in the travel business; while a website that acts as a discussion forum for mothers, like Mumsnet, will advertise pushchairs and children's clothes. If you don't have your own dedicated ad sales team, there are organizations that will help you find the most suitable advertisers for your site. Sideways News attracts ethically minded consumers, so it is especially important to find ads that are the right fit. 'We have arrangements with the Guardian Green Network, and also with Ethical Junction, an organization that brings publishers like ourselves together with advertisers.'

The second revenue stream that is worth considering is e-commerce. You could make a deal with another website that provides a service, such as price comparison, energy switching, internet dating or TV listings. The Sideways News site carries links to companies providing the latter two. When people click on the link it takes them to the partner organization's site, which shares the revenue generated with Sideways News.

A third way of generating income is to syndicate your content. This is especially useful if your site carries photographs and images that other people may want to use, or for sites that carry journalistic pieces, like Sideways News.

However, you should remember that if you are selling-on other people's work, you have to consider copyright issues. Unless you have their permission and have made a contract that allows you to sell the work, copyright remains with the creator, and they could sue you. How you pay the content provider, and the wording of the contract, will have to be carefully thought through before you start cutting syndication deals.

A fourth possible revenue stream may come from partnership deals. These are where you form a close relationship with an outside organization and provide a full-service package to them. For instance: Sideways News setting up a relationship with WRAP, the Waste Resource Action Programme, could work really well. The latter are a governmental scheme in the UK that advises businesses on waste management and recycling. Again, this is a perfect fit with the affluent ethical consumers Sideways News attracts. Not only does the deal give the partner organization a space on the website, but Sideways News could actively highlight the programme by promoting discussion forums on the subject within their community and writing advertorials about their latest campaigns. In return, the organization pays a fixed monthly fee for a set number of months, until the partnership deal expires. Sideways News have set up similar partnership deals, for example with Riverford organic foods, again spot on in terms of target audience match.

The great plus about 'selling' information in this way is that you are making money without having to bother with checkouts or payment and delivery systems. You can develop your site and your service at your own pace, and with patience and dedication you could eventually develop a brand that becomes known all over the world.

'Don't be afraid to start small,' says Emiel. 'Take it step by step. My advice? You have to go for it and really believe in it and always keep thinking and be creative! For example: we recently changed our business model to become a social bookmarking site – aggregating news articles submitted by users. We found writing all our own content too expensive and in this way we get a much higher user interaction. It goes to show that you always have to keep thinking, be flexible and be quick to adapt!

TOP TIPS

- Try to find something no one else is doing, but above all you must be passionate about your content.

- Research your target audience so that you know your core consumers, to entice advertisers and partners.

- It doesn't matter how 'niche' the subject matter is – there will always be someone interested in reaching your set of consumers.

- Test your content and seek feedback.

- Be prepared to change things and hone your website.

- Select the best possible team to back you up.

- Make sure you recruit the right advertisers who won't alienate your target audience.

Don't stop at selling advertising space – find e-commerce partners.

 Set up syndication deals with your content providers.

 Build up the site gradually until you have established a unique brand.

QUESTION

 How do you stop other people exploiting and making money out of your content without paying you for it?

No one has yet found an acceptable and foolproof way of policing the internet, and so content theft remains a perennial problem. But you can take steps to make it more difficult for people to download and use images from your site – for instance, by 'watermarking' them. If you discover that another website has reused your content in a way you don't like, contact them directly and explain why you are unhappy. Often people have borrowed thoughtlessly without understanding why it might upset the creator. They will often prove willing to remove the item from their site if you explain in reasonable terms why they should. But if they persistently steal content and refuse to remove it, complain to their internet service provider, who may be helpful and take the site down if you explain your case.

ACTIVITY

Identify your specialist interest – the one commodity the internet thrives on more than any other is information. Your specialist interest may be a particular sport, for instance, and you can then set up a site to provide news and a discussion forum for like-minded fans. Or perhaps you have a collection of crop-circle photographs that would attract other enthusiasts all over the world, or you might want to share information on a particular medical condition. Once you have a specialist interest, there are ways of generating revenue streams from the most esoteric information.

CHAPTER 7
SELLING LEADS

As we saw in the previous chapter, an information website offers many possibilities of generating income by selling space or links to other organizations. The most exciting aspect of e-commerce is that it is at its most effective a vast interconnected web – literally! – for which the saying 'You scratch my back, I'll scratch yours' could have been coined. Indeed, there is money to be made simply from brokering business needs and selling something you don't actually have yourself on behalf of other people.

How does it work? The other week, I was having a drink with a friend of mine who is a landscape gardener. Our conversation was interrupted several times as his mobile phone kept pinging to let him know another text message had arrived.

'You're popular,' I said. 'What's that – half a dozen messages in the last half hour? New girlfriend?'

'Business,' he replied. 'They're all leads. I subscribe to a service that picks up possible jobs for me online. When someone goes onto a particular garden design website, they can click to say they're interested in a quotation for work from a local landscaper. They type in their postcode, and if it's in my area, the website alerts me by text that someone could be looking for my services. Weekends, when people are on the internet and thinking about their gardens, my phone keeps pinging all the time. I make contact, arrange to visit and quote – I've picked up quite a few good contracts that way.'

Selling leads to other organizations is a new and profitable business created with the rise of the internet. You'll be familiar with the price comparison websites that now dominate the insurance market, or help you find the cheapest energy supplier or broadband provider. These are businesses that turn a handsome profit from brokering business needs. But there are still opportunities for the start-up, if you can tap into the right area.

In this chapter you will learn:

- the different kinds of sites that are selling leads;
- how content attracts consumers who can be passed on to your partner websites;
- the openings that still exist in this highly profitable field!

CASE STUDY

Nicola Gammon and ShootGardening

Nicola Gammon had a problem. She had a small garden in London that was full of dying plants. 'My trouble was that I impulse-bought plants at the garden centre, but didn't understand how important it was to put the right plant in the right place. Or I'd throw away the plant tags that were pushed down the side of the pot, because I thought it looked tacky leaving them on the plant, and then I couldn't remember what kind of plant I had or how to look after it, and couldn't look that up because I'd forgotten its name! They didn't all die, of course, but then I'd find myself faced with a rampant wisteria that needed pruning, and when I got around to looking it up in a plant book, I'd find that this was completely the wrong time of year to do so.

I remember saying to someone "How on earth am I supposed to remember that you prune the wisteria in February?"'

So Nicola's idea was a web-based service that would help take care of all that for you. A Californian by birth who had spent most of her career in credit derivatives trading and in fashion PR, she was keen to start her own online business. Out of her hobby – 'I have to be honest, I'm no horticulturalist, but I am passionate about gardening' – grew ShootGardening.co.uk. It contains first and foremost a huge database of 11,000 plants that draws people to the site. Many different varieties of every species are illustrated, and each plant's listing contains detailed information about where and how to plant it – chalky or acid soil, clay or loam, whether it likes sun or shade, the best aspect for it, its hardiness and so on. All this is free for anyone to access at the moment.

But for a small annual subscription, visitors are encouraged to join up as a member. Keen gardeners can list the plants in their own garden on the site and receive monthly e-mail reminders about what they should be doing with them. ShootGardening also uses Twitter and Facebook for plant updates. It's a clever and personalized version of those advice columns in magazines headed 'This month in your garden...' – only the advice you receive is bespoke, tailored to your own garden. It's also a gallery where proud gardeners can display photos of their backyards, and it boasts a garden design package that won an award from *Gardening Which?* magazine, beating similar design tools offered by leading landscaping companies and the BBC. Every month 140,000 people visit the site, and there are 13,000 members with 100 more joining every day. There is a real sense of an online community that shares a passion for plants.

Nicola also sells business membership via subscription. Costing only slightly more, this entitles horticultural profes-sionals to a listing on the site. There are categories for garden designers, landscape gardeners, tree surgeons and garden maintenance companies within the site's directory of services. So the directory doubles both as a source of revenue for the site and an additional resource that attracts more people to visit the site if they are looking for professional help with their garden.

For an extra charge, professionals can take out 'full business membership', which entitles them to enrol all their own clients on the site as ordinary members for a year for free, and thereby receive monthly care advice by e-mail once the designer or landscaper has created their new garden. The idea is that these client members then take out a subscription of their own once the year is up.

So far so good – but Nicola needed to attract more people to her site so that they would sign up to a subscription. She decided to use affiliate marketing to expand her online presence.

She contacted other like-minded gardening websites and persuaded them to put a banner ad for her site on theirs, with a link for people to click to take them straight to ShootGardening. co.uk, with a small discount if they sign up for membership. Some websites are happy to do this for free because they like Nicola's approach; others charge a commission. Nicola works out a valuation dependent on the size of the affiliate site's community, and gives them a commission with a code for their use, which tracks the number of click-throughs.

'We don't invest in marketing and PR; we knew that we had a group of people who are passionate about what we do and so it was a logical and low-cost way of extending our network,' she says. 'The affiliate marketing seems to work best where the partner site has put together an article around the subject matter. For instance, a couple of our members who have their own website based around their award-winning Victorian house garden in Bristol say "We really love this site", and that works so much better than a banner ad by itself.'

The terminology for what Nicola is doing with her site is 'brokering business needs' or 'becoming an affiliate'.

'At its simplest, the idea is to create a website that attracts people who are surfing the internet to come and look at it, and then as a result be inspired to move on to the partner website, where they make a purchase of goods or services', says Mark Harnett, an expert in online commerce. 'Or, in Nicola's case, vice versa, because she is using her links with other websites to draw people to hers. It's a cheap way of marketing your own site. Then, in addition, she's selling leads to other businesses by persuading them to subscribe as a business member.'

Within the basic business model, there can be many variations of the relationship between websites and their partners. Indeed, how far you choose to base your website on the business of selling leads is up to you.

There are some websites that have come about in a spirit of generosity because, first and foremost, their creator wants to share their expertise. These may sell the odd lead or two in order to cover running costs, but their primary purpose is to make the world more informed, rather than generate leads. (Of course, there may be other reasons for their existence too, such as to promote the 'brand' of their creator, if it happens to be the website of a TV or radio pundit!)

Others, like Nicola's, stand more firmly in the commercial camp, and their sole reason for being is to generate income for themselves and business for other businesses.

At the most basic, these may offer little content apart from lists of affiliated enterprises or tradespeople. Into this category fall the business directories and most of the price comparison sites – which usually do not compare all prices, of course, but only those of companies who pay them a commission for leads!

In between are a number of sites bridging the two, offering informational content and making a profit by directing visitors onwards to other companies' websites. These are often among the most successful kind, because they use their content to attract consumers who might not have imagined themselves yet at the point of purchase, but who are prompted to seek more information from the partner company's website, get a quote or buy, because the content has aroused in them the recognition that they are ready to do so.

So you can do as much or as little lead generation as you choose. For people who want to run a non-commercial site that reflects an interest or their passion, it can be a useful way of covering costs. At the other end of the scale, it can be a very profitable business indeed!

CONTENT

Decide first whether you want yours to be a straight listings/directory site, or one that promotes itself by offering 'expert' advice content. Either type can be successful, but the information-and-advice type of site can be especially attractive to prospective partners.

For example, imagine a website that specializes in information about health insurance. It offers articles about the different kinds available, and about what you should consider before deciding what kind of policy to buy. It also lists different policies from different companies and compares prices. On the page will be a button that says *Click to find quotes* or *Buy health insurance*. When the consumer clicks, the insurance company pays the site for a lead or an application.

Equally profitable could be the health website that contains information about different medical conditions. Someone looking for information on eczema, say, lands on the website because they have Googled the word 'eczema' or maybe 'dry itchy skin'. On the site they can read an article about the symptoms and treatment of the condition. At the top or the side of the page are ads for emollient creams or complementary therapies, and if the consumer clicks on these to visit the advertiser's website, again the broker website will be paid for the lead.

Be as creative as you can in designing the content for your site. Think about what kind of information people want, and how that relates to the business of your partner websites. Good content is what will attract people to your site, and keep them there long enough to be tempted to click on your partner's link. The internet is all about information sharing, and consumers very often begin their search for a product or a service by looking for content that will help them make an informed choice. So a person who has rising damp in their property or an infestation of wood-boring insects will begin by wanting to find out more about the problem. Once they feel sufficiently informed, they will be ready to look for a company that can solve it for them.

Getting the content exactly right is essential, for it is your ability to demonstrate that you can attract the right kind of consumers to your site that will win you business partners!

WHAT KINDS OF PARTNER BUSINESSES GENERATE THE BEST INCOME FOR YOUR SITE?

The more valuable the product, the more you will get paid for the lead. If your website calls a consumer to buy a new car, or take out a mortgage, or apply for a place on a college course, the rewards are greater. But there are already many big companies in the field who target the obviously profitable deals, and if you went for these you would find yourself up against stiff competition. So for a start-up, it's better to tap into an area where the rewards are initially smaller but there will be fewer competitors. Indeed, there are even websites that offer comparison information on the best kind of retractable washing line to buy!

'You need to specialize in something,' says Mark Harnett. 'Perhaps a particular kind of cooking implement or a particular gardening tool. Something that there will still be plenty of people searching for, but that is niche enough not to attract too much competition from the big guys.'

So let's suppose you are planning to set up a hypothetical website called What Hoe? (Sadly for budding entrepreneurs this particular web address is already taken and will direct you to an existing site specializing in a wide range of horticultural implements!)

You will need content that attracts consumers to the site, discussing the advantages and disadvantages of different types of hoe. What is the best hoe for a tall person? Which company makes hoes for less able gardeners, or gardeners with small hands? Do you need a different hoe for different soil types? And so on. Perhaps you might also include an article by a well-known gardening expert. Make sure, though, that you have permission to use it, and that the expert in question is willing for their name to appear on your site, if you are copying an article from another source!

In order to attract people to your site, you will need to make use of adwords so that your site rises high on the list of possible websites when someone Googles 'hoe' (for more information on how to do this, see *A Quick Start*

Guide to Google Adwords, published by Kogan Page). You could put a video of someone demonstrating hoeing techniques on YouTube, or buy ads on Facebook or other websites.

In this way, an interdependent web of e-commerce is created throughout the internet, with partnerships evolving between many different types of site. Remember, you need as many clicks as possible to keep your partners happy, so use your ingenuity to explore as many ways as you can of creating noteworthy content and marketing it to reach the right kind of consumers for your partners' businesses.

HONESTY IS THE BEST POLICY

There is a careful path to be steered when setting up a comparison website of this sort. Online commerce, as you have read before in this book, is based above all else on trust. So the information you offer on a comparison website has to be seen to be trustworthy! If you make claims that the 'best' garden hoe is Brand A, because Brand A happens to be paying you more for a five-star rating than Brand B, who only get four stars, you run the risk of being caught out. E-consumers are learning fast, and will usually look at more than one site. They are learning to discriminate between advertorial and genuine consumer reviews. You have been warned! It is important to make the content on your site as unbiased and as truthful as you can, and you might even consider including a page for consumers to leave their own reviews of products mentioned on the site. In this way the consumer feels they have visited a genuine comparison site, and are being invited to make up their own mind rather than having a particular product pushed at them.

GROWING YOUR LEADS BUSINESS

'There are lots of people who make a very good living out of this,' says Mark Harnett. 'And once you get good at it and have built a website that works, you don't have to put much effort into keeping it going – it virtually runs itself. So then you can think about doing multiple websites of a similar kind, with leads to other affiliated businesses, and make an income stream off each. Those websites will be your brand, all linked, driving yet more traffic between them.'

This is the business model adopted by the biggest players in the field. But with so many already exploiting the most obvious opportunities, realistically how much is left for new entrants to the business of selling leads?

'Surprisingly, most lead generation is still not done online,' says Mark Harnett. 'There is definitely an opportunity to find businesses that are not doing as much online as they could. Many companies are still relying on local advertising in traditional media to generate leads, or a large sales force on the road. You need to look for small upwardly moving enterprises of that kind, and set up a private deal with them to expand their business online.'

TOP TIPS

 Find a niche where you can offer expertise.

 Look for partner businesses that marry well with the kind of content you can present.

 Design compelling content that will attract the right kind of consumers.

 Use adwords and other means of online advertising to bring people to your site.

 Make your website known for its trustworthiness.

 Choose partner businesses that are not yet fully exploiting online opportunities.

 Offer prime rates for an exclusive deal.

QUESTION

 Should I start by designing the content for my site, then looking for partners, or should I begin by finding partners and tailoring the content to suit them?

The old chicken-and-egg question! There is no straightforward answer to this. Both processes really need to unfold simultaneously – as you find partners their input may alter the content you had planned, and as your content evolves, so you may find new areas of partnership. As with any serious business project, your first move is to analyse the potential market, which in this case comprises both possible partners and the consumers you wish to attract to the site. That is, unless you're planning the kind of website that simply reflects your personal interests and you aren't too concerned about making a profit! So you should do your research first, test the market, and let your findings dictate the direction your online business takes. But remember also that the most successful businesses are based on the passion of their creators, so there is little point in selling leads in an area of business that doesn't particularly interest you!

ACTIVITY

What is the most valuable product that you have the skill to sell? The more valuable the product, the more you will get paid for the lead. If your website calls a consumer to buy a new car, or take out a mortgage, or apply for a place on a college course, the rewards are greater. If you can discover a valuable product that is not already selling online, you are set to make serious money.

CHAPTER 8
SELLING IN A VIRTUAL WORLD:
HOW TO MAKE YOUR CREATIVITY PAY ON SOCIAL NETWORK SITES

The internet is an exciting place, full of opportunities for creative people. As well as physical products, you can sell virtual ones, and get paid in virtual money – which can be turned into hard cash in the real world.

One of the great successes of recent years is the rise of internet gaming, and in particular social networking games sites like Second Life and IMVU, where people take on different characters or 'avatars', and enjoy a separate existence in a virtual world. You can be whoever you want to be, live in the kind of home you've always dreamed of, change your looks at will, meet and interact with other people, and – most interesting for the budding online entrepreneur – *shop* online to furnish your apartment or dress in style.

It's a bit like dressing-up games for grown-ups – though there are now also virtual life sites catering for younger teenagers and children too. These sites are for people to have fun and indulge their fantasies, but there are also money-making opportunities here. Although transactions take place in the virtual world, the most successful games players are making real money out of designing virtual products – some of them reportedly earning as much as fashion designers in the real world.

Want to have a go? It's a fun way of selling online, and who knows, you could strike lucky and become a Valentino of a virtual world.

In this chapter you will learn:

- the sites to look out for;

- how to make pocket money from your creations that you can spend onsite;

- the way to create a look that earns you significant wealth in the real world too.

CASE STUDY

Spike Sieghardt, games player

Spike Sieghardt doesn't give away much about himself – his real self, that is. He allowed us to know that he was born in Minnesota, USA, and lives in the Twin Cities. Everything else about him – age, past career, hair colour – is a blank, and he likes to keep it that way, though he did let slip that he had done a college course in graphic design, and worked with CAD software.

'The thing that always appealed to me about the internet is that you can be whoever you want to be,' says Spike. 'I've been involved in the online gaming community for years. But it wasn't until I came across Second Life that I really felt at home – my second home, of course! I could create an entire new being for myself – one of many, if I felt like it. I could be a poet, a rock star, a high-rolling banker, an assassin, even a woman if the fancy took me.'

Spike was fascinated by the different looks he could create for himself. As well as Second Life, he registered as a social networking player on a site called IMVU.

'It's one of the easiest to use if you're a creator,' he says. 'When you first enter the site, you choose a name for yourself, and a basic avatar, and they give you 1,000 free credits to shop for clothes to individualize your look. But that's only the beginning. As soon as you start playing seriously, you personalize everything – body type, hair style and colour, the clothes you wear, your online home, your wheels. You sign up for an online account and credits to spend in virtual shops. After a while you get to know the designers that create the looks you like, and you go back to their carts over and over. You wouldn't believe it from my avatar, but in real life I'm kind of a dull dresser – jeans, T-shirt, loafers – but online I like to let rip. At first I was into that Eighties Kiss look – monochrome make-up and jump suits. When I couldn't find stuff exactly the way I wanted it, I began designing my own online outfits, and the people I was interacting with on the site started asking where they could buy similar styles. So I started selling to them.'

At first Spike just made a few credits here and there, which he spent on the site. But as he grew more confident, he broadened his range of designs.

'I got heavily into more Goth looks,' he says. 'Somehow that struck a chord, and word spread. I was selling a lot to online vampires. Before long I was picking up more credits than I could spend online, and I started converting them to real money.' He's cagey about what he actually earns from selling online designs. 'It's nowhere near as much as the big guys, who make hundreds of thousands of dollars a year. But put it this way, it's more than I earn from my day job.'

HOW DO YOU FOLLOW SPIKE'S EXAMPLE?

'It's a growing field,' says Mark Harnett, director of marketing at IMVU. 'There are quite a few social networking games sites now, and on ones like ours and Second Life people are spending and making money. Part of the fun of the game is selecting your avatar's look, and we have over 4 million items in our catalogue. Anything you can imagine, it's there to buy online – clothes, hairstyles, eye colours, skin colour, make-up, jewellery, tattoos, furniture, rooms...'

Any means of expressing yourself in a virtual world is available. The reason IMVU's catalogue is so big is that almost all of the items in it are created by individual site users, who sell their virtual designs to other site users. They sell under their avatar names, so if a buyer sees something they like in the catalogue, they know who has created it and they can search in future for that creator's cart. Each seller earns credits, which they can use online or sell on to convert to real money.

In other words, IMVU has created a whole virtual economy.

It helps if you have a graphics or computer-aided design background, but it's by no means necessary. 'There are more than 100,000 creators on IMVU who are creating things,' says Mark. 'Most people do it at a hobbyist level because it's fun to create new room colours or T-shirt designs – that's pretty straightforward. A handful at the top are making a lot of money – many of them 3D graphic arts people who are able to create unbelievably realistic images.'

As with so many other online enterprises, the key is to work with what you love. If you care about your product and put enthusiasm and energy into it, other people will care too and buy it. Cynics need not apply.

FINDING YOUR NICHE

But how do you make the leap from small-time site user selling to friends, to top-flight designer making serious money?

The trick is to follow Spike's example and find a niche market that helps you establish a reputation among enthusiasts. You should search for a corner of the market that will be yours – a look and style that you like yourself, and that will allow you to express your creativity.

'You have to go and play on the world first and find your niche,' says Mark. 'Then you can go on to create products that satisfy the demand for that niche. It might be bikers and leather and tattoos, or it might be disco neon. There are many different niche communities on sites like IMVU, and they are willing to buy a lot of stuff, if you can create looks that appeal to them.'

Don't be afraid of starting small. You shouldn't spread yourself too thinly by struggling to create a huge and varied portfolio of designs. You will do much better to start off with a few unusual items that will appeal to like-minded people.

Once you have established a reputation, then you can really let your imagination loose. The virtual world is your oyster!

TOP TIPS

 Play on the site until you understand how it works.

 Start small and simple.

 Sell to your friends first – let them help you create a reputation.

 Find your niche.

 Sell what you love.

 Build on your successes – don't be content with pocket money, but see if you can attract a wider following for your designs.

QUESTION

 What if I suspect someone else on the site is ripping off my ideas?

Welcome to the real world of fashion! Internationally acclaimed designers like Ralph Lauren or Jasper Conran have faced exactly the same problem when High Street imitators or sweatshops in the developing world steal their ideas. It's hard to copyright designs, because a design thief can so easily claim that what they have created is not identical. Sometimes it is best to remember the old adage 'Imitation is the sincerest form of flattery.' People copying your designs can actually enhance your reputation.

The beauty of the online community is that selling online is all about reputation and feedback. Word will soon spread that you have an imitator and if your designs are good and you continue to stay ahead of the game, your fans will stick by you.

ACTIVITY

Start playing! Yes, your activity is to play in the virtual world as much as you can so that you can find a corner of the market that will be yours and thus develop a look and style that will allow you to express your creativity. Then you can sell your style to your virtual friends.

CHAPTER 9
IF AT FIRST YOU DON'T SUCCEED; AN ONLINE MILLIONAIRE'S STORY

Throughout this book, you've seen examples of how people have exploited online technology to sell anything from the treasures in their attic to information. The beauty of an online business is that start-up costs need not be enormous, and the internet offers the chance to grow the business as big as you like, or to stay small and select if you prefer.

Fortune favours the bold, however, and as well as drawing together the threads of the lessons you'll have learned so far, our final chapter is about the very real rewards that online selling can bring. It features the inspiring story of a man who was disillusioned with his corporate career. He took the brave step of resigning to start his own business, and eventually became a multimillionaire through a simple but clever online sales proposition. It didn't happen overnight, but through good times and bad he never lost faith in his idea, and in the end it paid off, many times over.

In this chapter you'll discover:

- how a niche proposition can become enormously profitable;
- why getting in early on a new idea is both a blessing and a curse;
- how some disadvantages can be turned into advantages;
- how to start local but finish global;
- and how to make your business so successful and attractive that your competitors want to buy you out!

CASE STUDY

Richard Coundley and his holiday rental site

In the early 1990s, Richard Coundley was working for one of the UK's biggest corporations in a high-powered job reporting directly to the company's treasurer. However, he was asked to step out of his position for six months and, as a member of a four-man team reporting directly to the chief executive, was tasked with developing a plan to downsize and redesign the very large overhead function of the company as part of the privatization process.

The project was a roaring success, and the board gratefully adopted the restructure plan. Richard and the rest of the team were told their work had been 'exceptional' and that exceptional performance deserved exceptional rewards. The London *Financial Times* ran a double-page spread on the restructuring, and the company's share price leapt. Unfortunately, Richard and his boss, the treasurer, did not always see eye to eye and when it came to his annual appraisal that year, to Richard's amazement his boss reduced his bonus for not having achieved his objectives in his old job, despite being seconded to work for the CEO.

While an appeal to the main board's HR director resolved the issue, Richard's disillusion with the corporate world had started. However, it was while managing an acquisition in the United States that the disillusionment crystallized with the realization that he was not good at company politics, and did not want to spend his life on an aeroplane and in a hotel room parted from his wife. And Richard wanted his performance to be judged by the marketplace rather than by a boss.

Meanwhile, he and his wife had recently invested in a holiday apartment in Ireland. 'We'd been staying with friends, and my wife was really keen to own one of the new apartments that were being built. It was her idea, not mine, but I wanted to keep her happy, so we used some savings, borrowed from her parents, and somehow scraped the money together.'

Their plan was to let the apartment for some of the year, to cover their costs, but when they advertised the apartment in *The Times* newspaper in the UK, there was little response. It started Richard wondering about how other owners and agents with similar holiday properties advertised their properties. He and his wife, Marcelle Speller, who had held board-level marketing jobs with international companies including American Express and Air UK, had been discussing setting up a small business of their own. After their disillusionment with the corporate world, they began making plans for a listing service for holiday property owners.

'All we wanted to do in the short to medium term was to create a business that would pay the bills,' says Richard. 'Initially we were thinking of a paper-based brochure or magazine – in other words, doing exactly what was already being done by other companies – which would have been an uphill task against established competition. But this was 1995, and I was becoming fascinated by the possibilities of the internet. I'd watched everything at work being networked, and realized that once a company or a society starts on that road, there is no retreat – it changes everything. It dawned on me that the web was going to be a great medium for advertising holiday lettings.'

When he and Marcelle analysed the potential of their business idea, they realized they could be onto even more of a winner than they'd thought. While existing paper-based publications were mainly focused on niche markets either by country or property type or both, there was no need to restrict the business to advertising only Irish holiday lettings, or even lettings in the British Isles. The existing market was surprisingly fragmented even at national level, let alone an international one. 'I could see there was a longer-term opportunity to consolidate. You could use the internet to build a business that would dominate the whole market for advertising holiday properties to rent and be global in scope.'

Richard's was a simple but brilliant idea. With a paper listings business, you are held back by the physical size of the product. No one wants a great thick telephone directory of a brochure to drop through their letterbox – even assuming it would fit! 'But with an online listings business, there is no limit to the size of the inventory. We could sell advertising space to people with holiday property all over the world, and offer holidaymakers the choice of hundreds of thousands of villas, apartments and cottages.'

Richard and Marcelle took the plunge in 1996 and set up the first online holiday property listings site in the UK. He sold space on the site for people to advertise their holiday properties for let. Revenue would be generated by charging a fixed fee – annual or six monthly – to the property owner or agent.

'There are both advantages and disadvantages to being early in the field,' he says. 'Yes, you're getting in first, and you're not running against entrenched competition. But the disadvantage is that it can take a long time to grow to a scale that generates profit. We were also launching in a new medium, using new and untried technology.'

When their listings service launched, it had just 15 properties on its books.

'It doesn't sound much, does it? But that's another way in which online scores over any other way of doing business. If you were publishing a paper-based holiday property magazine, it wouldn't be viable. But online you can afford to start small and add to your inventory incrementally, because once you've spent the money to get the website up and running, the costs of adding another property, and then another, and then more, are actually quite low.'

But it wasn't enough, as we have already learned, simply to put up a website and hope people stumbled across it. Somehow Richard had to market the site. And these were such early days for online businesses that nobody really knew how it could be done. 'Again, that's both a disadvantage and an advantage', he says. 'We didn't know how to market online, but neither did our competitors. The big corporates were slow off the mark and web illiterate in the early days. The successful guy is the one who learns fastest – the good problem solver, if you like.'

Richard, with a degree in engineering and an MBA from the London Business School, had a background in problem solving, and Marcelle had an MBA from INSEAD. Nonetheless, the first few years were hard. Holiday property letting was seen as a niche within the wider travel market, and so it was impossible for him to win any venture capital – investors at the time were too busy looking for mainstream opportunities. So it took faith, and staying power, through the lean years.

But sometimes, Richard says, it actually helps that you don't have much money. 'For a start, there won't be too much competition in the field, because no one else can raise capital either. And if you're strapped for cash, there is only one way to survive: to be smart. Some of the well-financed internet start-ups were lazy. They had the money to go to the advertising agencies, and they just blew it – ie handed the agencies hundreds of thousands of pounds for campaigns that didn't work. The agencies at the time did not know how to market online. We had to look for other ways of marketing ourselves – and that was when I made the big discovery that search engines were the key to success online.'

Richard knew he had to market his business to two different groups: those who owned holiday property, and those who wanted to rent it. 'Back in 1996 it wasn't at all clear how you would reach customers online – whether it would be through traditional routes like newspaper and TV advertising, or using web-based directories or some kind of internet portal. The breakthrough idea came when I went to talk to potential customers and discovered that everyone wanted their search to be simple – to type what they needed into a box and hit *Find*. They wanted to use search engines. Today it seems obvious, but it was not clear then whether directories (eg Yahoo), search engines (eg Google), portals or traditional media would be the way to reach the customers. So I put my efforts into finding ways to make our website rise high on the list of results that appeared when someone typed in any of the many possible search phrases, eg 'holiday let in Spain'.

Richard understood what many others in the field did not at the time, and so became one of the first to realize the potential of exploiting search engine technology to grow his business. By optimizing for the search engines, he clawed an advantage over the competition, and as the use of the internet steadily increased in the UK, the business gained momentum. The more people came to his site to look for a holiday let, the more holiday rental property owners were attracted to buy space on it. Now money was starting to flow back in as the business achieved a critical mass. Marcelle's background in traditional marketing helped secure vital PR coverage in prestigious national newspapers, and the links to their business, Holiday-Rentals, also helped increase the site's rankings in the search engines.

'If you look at any listing business, you'll realize that size really matters. There are economies of scale, which are critical to profitability. As the business grows, unit costs go down, your revenue increases and mostly importantly your profit per listing increases as well. But there is also what I call "competitive advantage of scope". In other words, if you attract someone to your website, you want to maximize the potential for them to actually find what they want and maximize the cost effectiveness of your marketing, by having as broad a selection on the site as possible. Once an online listing business gets past the break-even point and continues growing, it has the potential to generate ever larger amounts of cash – particularly if it dominates the marketplace.'

All the long hours Richard and his wife had put in to the business were at last paying off. From the early days others attempted to copy what he had done, and 'me-too' holiday rentals sites were always springing up online. But Holiday-Rentals.com had been first and always the largest in the UK. It had also carved an advantage over the competition by developing an integrated web-based platform to run the whole business, including handling the online marketing, advertiser data and photo upload, payments, invoicing, subscriptions renewal, and even revenue accounting. As a result, a company in Germany with the same business model approached Holiday-Rentals, wanting access and the business was able to rent out use of this system and make money as an applications service provider.

Indeed, the enterprise was so successful that Richard eventually pulled off the coup that everyone in business envies – having made his fortune from selling, he then made even more money by selling the company!

'Right from the start, I had believed there was an opportunity to consolidate the holiday lettings business on a global basis. A company in Austin, Texas, had similar ambitions, and they had raised the venture capital to snap up competitors in the

United States. But, as they lacked the technology platform that we had designed and built, they accelerated their plans to make an acquisition in Europe and came up with an offer we simply couldn't refuse.'

Richard became a multimillionaire overnight. Better still, because he believed in the acquiring company's global strategy, he was canny enough to take a proportion of the payment in shares as well as retaining a seat on the board. As a result he has made money again from the success of the company that acquired his. He has an enviable lifestyle, and the satisfaction of having achieved his dream.

LESSONS FROM RICHARD'S STORY

Richard's story is an inspiring one. But what lessons could you take from it?

First, don't be afraid to start small. At the same time as the internet offers all the scope of an enormous inventory, it also allows you to launch with a tiny one, as Richard found. You can take your time to build the business as you discover what people are most interested in buying from you, and although it is worth doing some market research first, once you are certain that there is a market for what you want to sell, be it a physical commodity or ideas or information or listings, don't delay. Once you have a good idea of how your site should look and the money to build it, go ahead. Although the initial outlay might seem steep, remember that unlike a paper-based business, the cost of adding items to your inventory can be minimal.

Second, find your niche. When Richard started his business, nobody was prepared to invest in what seemed only a tiny part of the wider travel business. But he proved them wrong, by growing a niche enterprise into a potentially global one. If you can find the right niche, there may well be opportunities of consolidating once the business starts to grow.

Being early in the field can be a massive advantage. That isn't to say that a 'me-too' company will fail, but you will have to work harder and be even more clever to find that competitive edge if there are already many others preceding you in the same market. On the other hand, the early starters will have made all the expensive mistakes, so you can learn from their experience – but to beat them you will need to find a twist that makes your business stand out.

Don't let lack of investment deter you. As Richard discovered, being short of cash can make you more creative than the opposition. Be prepared to think outside the box, and you may latch onto the next Big Idea.

Times may well be hard in those early months. You will very probably have to work long hours and, as Richard found, it will feel as if you are pouring money into a bottomless pit. 'All we ever seemed to do was stick money into the business, with nothing coming out: investing, investing, investing.' What kept him going? 'Just a refusal to give up, really. Keeping faith in your idea is essential.'

Once the business takes off, make sure you keep growing your inventory to take advantage as Richard did of that 'competitive advantage of scope'. You want to be sure that your website becomes known as the one where people will find what they are looking for in your market – just as eBay or Amazon have done in the wider marketplace. Being competitive in price is helpful, but remember the lesson Richard learned from his early meetings with potential customers: online, people like the search process to be simple and may go no further than the site that carries the bigger range.

Again, it's all about reputation – and in this case that meant generating enquiries and bookings for advertisers. The reward was that a significant proportion of new advertisers came because of personal recommendations from existing advertisers. Never underestimate the power of viral marketing, particularly with the rise of social networking.

Be creative in the way you approach technology. Good systems have the power to both increase revenue and decrease your operating costs. If you can develop one that is scalable and superior to your competitors', they will want to join with you, and you may be able to generate income from selling or leasing your technology to others.

Finally, don't be afraid to think big. Richard freely admits that though he was looking for a way of paying the bills at the start, he was also bold enough to think ahead to the long term and spot the possibilities for growing his business globally – another advantage of selling online.

SOME ADVICE FROM RICHARD

What advice does Richard have for people thinking of starting an online sales enterprise?

'Someone once asked me *how* I became an entrepreneur,' says Richard. 'But the "How", while not easy, is straightforward – you start a business. Another important question is about motivation, in other words the *why*. If the answer is that you really want to run a business, you hunger to try out ideas, to be your own boss, to let the marketplace judge your performance rather than your boss, to follow your dream, go ahead and do it. You'll never look back.'

TOP TIPS

Start small, but think big.

Look for a niche that has not been properly exploited.

Don't let lack of investment hold you back – think of creative solutions to marketing problems.

Keep the faith in your dream, and don't give up too soon.

Expand your inventory to dominate the market.

Reputation, as always online, is key. You need to become known not only for good prices and great service, but also for a wide range, so that people know they will find what they want on your site.

Look for ways of being creative with technology, so you can sell your business solutions to others.

Sell up when you've exhausted the possibilities of getting more enjoyment from your business, and enjoy the proceeds of your labours!

QUESTION

What is the secret of making profits online?

Keep expanding your business. In the online world and in the listing business, it is size that matters. There are economies of scale, which are critical to profitability. Your unit costs go down, your profitability goes up. Once an online business gets past the tipping point, it will make more and more money as you grow to dominate the marketplace and dominate the search engines.

With over 1,000 titles in printed and digital format, **Kogan Page** offers affordable, sound business advice

www.koganpage.com

You are reading one of the thousands of books published by **Kogan Page**. As Europe's leading independent business book publishers **Kogan Page** has always sought to provide up-to-the-minute books that offer practical guidance at affordable prices.

KoganPage